A Home for Gori

OTHER LOTUS TITLES

Ajit Bhattacharjea	*Sheikh Mohammad Abdullah: Tragic Hero of Kashmir*
Amarinder Singh	*The Last Sunset: The Rise and Fall of the Lahore Durbar*
Anil Dharker	*Icons: Men & Women Who Shaped Today's India*
Alam Srinivas & TR Vivek	*IPL: The Inside Story*
Duff Hart Davis	*Honorary Tiger*
M.J. Akbar	*Byline*
M.J. Akbar	*Blood Brothers: A Family Saga*
Maj. Gen. Ian Cardozo	*Param Vir: Our Heroes in Battle*
Madhu Trehan	*Tehelka as Metaphor*
Mushirul Hasan	*Knowledge, Power and Politics*
Nayantara Sahgal (ed.)	*Before Freedom: Nehru's Letters to His Sister*
Nilima Lambah	*A Life Across Three Continents*
Psyche Abraham	*From Kippers to Karimeen*
Robert Hutchison	*The Raja of Harsil: The Legend of Frederick 'Pahari' Wilson*
Ruskin Bond	*Green Book*
Saad Bin Jung	*Wild Tales from the Wild*, foreword by Mansur Ali Khan, Nawab of Pataudi
Sharmishta Gooptu and Boria Majumdar (eds)	*Revisiting 1857: Myth, Memory, History*
Shashi Tharoor & Shaharyar M. Khan	*Shadows Across the Playing Field*
Shrabani Basu	*Spy Princess: The Life of Noor Inayat Khan*
Shyam Bhatia	*Goodbye Shahzadi: A Political Biography*
Sunil Gupta	*Living on the 'Adge' in JhandeWalan Thompson*
Susan Visvanathan	*The Children of Nature: The Life and Legacy of Ramana Maharshi*
Verghese Kurien (As told to Gauri Salvi)	*I Too Had a Dream*
Zubin Mehta	*The Score of My Life*

FORTHCOMING TITLES

Bill Ricquier	*The Pakistani Masters*
Michel De Grece	*The Bourbon Rajah*
M.J. Akbar	*Have Pen, Will Travel*

HABIB REHMAN (S.S.H. Rehman) was born, brought up and educated in Hyderabad. He began his career with the Indian army, which he left as a Major to join the hospitality business, and has spent three decades with ITC.

Rehman has extensively researched Indian cuisine and re-created it in a modern context, helping generate global awareness of its nuances and variety. ITC-Welcomgroup restaurants, many of which Rehman has helped set up, are considered icons in the world of international cuisine.

In the mid-nineties, his wife unexpectedly brought a pup home and set off a series of events that Rehman could hardly have foreseen. This recounting of the story of that pet, Gori, also includes important milestones of his career, which he capped when he retired recently as director-in-charge of ITC's hotels, travel and tourism, and food businesses.

Rehman continues to be a well-regarded figure in the hospitality industry. He lives in Delhi in his new home, which is a tribute to the architectural legacy of the city, and a memorial to Gori.

KISHORE SINGH first met Habib Rehman at the start of his career three decades ago as a travel writer for magazines in India and abroad. He continued that association as chief editor with a leading publishing house, as well as editor of a weekend supplement for a financial newspaper. In between, he launched a couple of lifestyle magazines, wrote scripts for documentary films, and wrote and edited books across a diverse range of subjects. He continues to be a newspaper columnist and currently heads exhibitions and publications for a Delhi-based arts institution.

A Home for Gori

Habib Rehman
with
Kishore Singh

Lotus Collection

First published in 2010
The Lotus Collection
An imprint of
Roli Books Pvt Ltd
M-75, G.K. II Market
New Delhi 110 048
Phone: ++91 (011) 4068 2000
Fax: ++91 (011) 2921 7185
E-mail: info@rolibooks.com; Website: rolibooks.com

Also at
Bangalore, Chennai, Jaipur, Mumbai & Varanasi

Layout Design: Naresh L. Mondal

ISBN: 978-81-7436-807-2

Typeset in Janson Text by Roli Books Pvt Ltd
and printed at Nutech Print Services, New Delhi.

Dedicated to my human
and canine families

Contents

Acknowledgements

This book has been with me for five years, a story that I knew had to be told, one of the reasons why I organized and preserved all records pertaining to Gori's life and illness. How I would tell the story, or when, was irrelevant.

One evening, in the course of a conversation, my friend Pramod Kapoor asked me why I had chosen to build a house in Panchsheel Park, the south Delhi residential colony, instead of the farmhouse I had hoped to treat myself to once I retired. I found myself telling him Gori's story and my promise that I would build a memorial in sight of where she lay buried. It was on Pramod's egging that I was able to turn what was a mere wish into reality. He put together an editorial team, and sooner than I had imagined, and coincidentally commemorating Gori's fifth death anniversary, we were able to publish the book.

Various people have contributed to this book with their memories, among them my step-daughter, Chandan, and step-granddaughter, Shagun. Gori's vet, Dr Pradeep Rana, gave freely of his time when asked to explain Gori's illness at some length, and interpret the many prescriptions he had written for her. Agnes, who was with us when Gori first arrived as a pup, filled in the gaps with her keen memory. John was available too, not just with stories and anecdotes but, in Gori's lifetime, to care for her and manage her frequent trips to the vet. To both of them, I owe a debt of thanks.

Were it not for Kishore Singh who captured the feelings that mirrored the intimate relationship I had with Gori, the depth and substance would have been lost. He deserves much more than an acknowledgment – my deepest gratitude indeed. The editor, Swati Chopra, worked hard to meet the deadline, for which I am grateful.

Prologue

27 July 2005

The rains had made the earth soft, so digging was not difficult. Not that we had to dig very deep. The grave was to be a shallow affair, hardly subterranean enough to shift the many layers of soil that lay piled on top of the thousands of Mongol soldiers who had, long ago, perished below the fourteenth century battlements of Allauddin Khilji's Siri Fort.

Under the shadow of those ruins, that evening, one more body would be interred, but unlike the Mongol warriors of fortune, it would not be an anonymous corpse. Gori was the love of my life, and she had died, only hours earlier, waiting for me to return home. Just that morning, I had pleaded with her vet to keep her alive long enough for her to die in my arms.

But death had cheated her, and me, of that privilege.

Almost ten years ago, to the day, she had come home as a puppy, only to be rejected by me. I had wanted nothing to do with her, had wanted her sent back, had even exiled her from the house. Gori, however, had not taken her abandonment to heart, in fact, had clawed her way back with growing affection, to build a stronger bond than I have ever experienced with another living being. And now she was gone, leaving me bereft.

Back at home, a mere stone's throw away, wrapped in her blanket and surrounded by her favourite toys, Gori's body awaited its funeral. I had come to love her with a fierce passion I had not known I was capable of. Now as I looked up from my exertions at the grove of *keekar* trees in the neighbourhood, I could see the rubble of the historical precinct giving way to the houses of N Block, Panchsheel Park.

The sky was leaden when her inert form was lowered into the grave. John and Agnes scattered soil over the wrapped form till there was nothing left of her. Earlier, I had sent Vishnu to the nursery for a sapling with which to mark her grave. As the tree was lowered into the ground, I looked at the corner house which, I could see, would have a perfect view of Gori's final resting place.

At that moment I knew exactly what I would do. However difficult it might be, I would pull down that corner house and rebuild it from scratch, a memorial to a dog who had blessed me with ten years of her life.

This, then, is Gori's story.

A Dog's Life

I do not recall any special affection I might have had for dogs in my childhood. If there were dogs in my friends' homes, I do not remember them. I must have played with them in their homes – it is impossible to believe that not one of them would have kept dogs – but at least there is no special memory attached to it. What I can safely say is that my own family never kept dogs, perhaps because my grandmother did not like them for the suggestion of impurity that Islam bestows on them. Nor do I remember the subject coming up for discussion, perhaps because we were used to other pets. There were pigeons, parrots, a pen with hens of all kinds, even an aquarium, in the sprawling house in Himayat Nagar in which I grew up in the '40s and '50s.

That house had been designed by Hashmat Raza, who was the first architect from Hyderabad to have qualified from the Royal Institute of British Architecture in London. With its huge front and back yards, it was ideal for our large and extended family that consisted of brothers and sisters and cousins who, when not at school, could be found playing cricket, or climbing trees, or doing the things children used to do then when elders didn't want them in the house, and the grounds provided sufficient space to keep us busy.

The first time in my life I became conscious of dogs was after I was commissioned into the Indian army. Following my training at the Indian Military Academy in Dehradun from 1963 to 1964, the pips of a second-lieutenant on my shoulder, hair trimmed, shoes polished to a fault, and my worldly belongings packed into a hold-all and trunk, after a short stint at the regimental centre in Sagar in Madhya Pradesh, I found myself at a picket called Hanker in the Himalayan outreaches of what is now known as Arunachal Pradesh, but was then known as NEFA, North East Frontier Agency.

Getting to Hanker, or even NEFA, in those days, was the stuff of safaris. The train from Hyderabad to Tinsukia, or to Dibrugarh, both railheads in Assam, took four days. From either place, a two-and-a-half-day military convoy would transport you ahead, from where Hanker post was another nine or ten days' march on foot. Nor did it hold too many attractions. Located at 11,000 feet and surrounded by hills denuded of vegetation on account of heavy snowfall and high winds, it lacked in charm for all but a yogi. Here, the commander and his men made their home in bunkers, which comprised accommodation assembled using mud walls, tarpaulin sheeting and bamboo screens, hardly adequate protection from the extreme weather. High mountains cut the sunlight short, as a result of which the days seemed shorter than the nights that stretched long and lonely.

This remote outpost was important because following the 1962 flash war with China, where we did not cover ourselves in glory, and as part of subsequent peace moves, it was agreed that both the Chinese and Indian armies would pull back to de-militarize the zone. In the absence of the regular army guarding the border, it was left to paramilitary forces to patrol and manage the frontiers, a task they were not quite prepared for. So, army officers were inducted into the Assam Rifles, which was how, in

1964, I found myself posted at Hanker, and a temporary mentor to Bullet.

Bullet had billeted himself to the Hanker picket. In the hundreds of pickets across the Himalayas you will find as many clones of Bullet. They are *gaddi* or *bhutia* mongrels, commonly spread across the mountains, who adopt a post and make it their home. Over time, they develop not just a relationship with the post commander and his platoon but become fierce and loyal guard dogs and part of the rhythm of a soldier's life. They also find themselves lavished by the affections of soldiers away from their loved ones.

I noticed Bullet almost immediately, when he came to offer his respects on my arrival at the base camp at Manigang, and then followed me to Hanker as the first occupants of that picket. He was a large but nondescript dog who soon developed a deep sense of ownership that others, as temporary occupants of that picket, did not have. He would soon get used to the movement of platoons from the post every fortnight. Hanker was a new picket, I was its first commander, and as a pack-dog, Bullet soon realized I was top dog. He simply attached himself to me, anointing himself second-in-command.

It might seem a strange name for a dog but Bullet more than lived up to it. After all, a bullet is a foot-soldier's best friend, or foe, and Bullet established that he could be both, depending on which side you belonged to! Then there was the romance of the Royal Enfield motorcycle, commonly referred to as 'Bullet', which was known for its reliability and ruggedness. Bullet would prove to be both.

When we began going out on night patrols, Bullet would be chained to keep him from following us. I fretted that his barking would alert the enemy and give away our position, so I eventually let him accompany us on the patrols. At first my concern was that his company on these night patrols might betray our presence to the Chinese forces, but soon enough realized that his canine senses were better attuned than ours at distinguishing friend from foe. He could not have reacted better than if he had been trained for the job. With little to do during the day other than strategizing our night patrols, I could observe Bullet dispassionately and soon discovered his ability to tell people apart based on their clothes and smell. The soldiers in their uniforms he recognized as part of the universe that he occupied. He also accepted without suspicion those who provided services to our camp – who supplied yak milk, for instance, or distributed the mail, or carried the rations. Anyone outside this circle of comfort would raise his suspicion and hackles, whether they were passing shepherds or those trekking between their distant village homes. No such stranger, whether hostile or polite, could come close to the post without Bullet pouncing on his trousers and holding him there, emitting a series of fierce growls till everyone was alerted and appropriate action taken.

I learned soon enough that instead of being wary, I needed to be thankful for Bullet's sharp night vision, acute hearing, and highly developed olfactory senses. He would warn us of the presence of other humans, or animals, with a cautionary bark. If we were tired, or didn't take him seriously, and he sensed danger, his bark would be sharp enough to get us to react. Bullet was a post- and patrol-dog, and proud of it.

During the day he hung around with the troops as though he were part of the pack. Typically for us, the day began with a stand-to, part of the morning exercise routine where we flexed our bodies and took a roll-call. The official part of the duties consisted of writing reports, sending dispatches, and attending to any administrative needs that, in our remote post, seemed laughable. If a day passed without somebody being bitten by snakes or falling ill from exposure to intense cold and frostbite, we put it down as a good one. More comfort than a sleeping bag was unimaginable, a bed an unheard-of luxury. In the afternoons, we'd play an occasional game of volleyball to keep the troops fit and in humour. On these occasions, Bullet would look on from the sidelines, probably wondering at the tribal nature of this jousting, every once in a while diving into the court to chase the ball, before finding himself evicted again.

The JCO (junior commissioned officer), or 'Sahib' as he is referred to in the Indian army, is the most important link between an officer and his troops, and keeps a hawk's eye on everything. A crucial link between the officer cadre and the non-commissioned officers (NCOs) and jawans, the JCO is possibly the most important and the most unremarked person in the hierarchy of the Indian army. They are also platoon commanders, and in a rifle company such as mine, the subaltern's position is interchangeable with the JCO's. I learned soon enough that the three most important people in my immediate orbit consisted of naturally the Sahib, my batman or orderly (now known as *sahayak*, helper), and my signaler, who would use the unsophisticated equipment issued to him to stay in touch with the base unit, transmitting signals.

It was clear that Bullet knew I was boss, and he gave me the deference he felt was my due. Having taken on the challenging responsibility of the picket's strength of some twenty-five occupants, he made sure that he routinely inspected the troops, acknowledging and even enjoying their affections. He'd enjoy the occasional back-rub, and wait outside the cook's tent to be fed. But when it was time to rest, you could count on it that he'd be outside my bunker. Not only did Bullet prove to be an invaluable companion, I learned first-hand why a dog is referred to as man's best friend. At 11,000 feet, stationed at a sensitive border, only twenty years old, far from home and mostly alone, Bullet was my new best friend.

A post commander's tenure at that time was usually for six months, while the men assigned to him changed every fortnight. For me, it was simply another task to welcome a new platoon, caution them about the peculiarities of that location and the movement of enemy troops, and brief them regarding my requirements. But I noticed that for Bullet, each time one platoon was replaced by the next, it meant rebuilding his relationships. He would have to forge new associations and new affections. The troops returned his friendliness easily enough, but while he took their comings and goings in his stride, it must have cost him a good deal to endear himself to another set of soldiers, and repeat the routine a fortnight later. Yet, he did this with a casual grace and, increasingly, with a sense of proprietorship – this was his spot high up in the mountains, and while they were free to come and go, he took pride in showing them around, joined the night patrols, and found solace among the more permanent residents of the camp, my batman and I.

It was in this milieu of partnerships that Kutty, my signaler, reminded me that it was Eid. On the evening before, he came up to me to ask what my programme for Eid was. Before this, I had not given any thought to Kutty's religion. In Kerala, which is where Kutty was from, the name could as easily belong to a Hindu or a Syrian-Christian as to a Muslim.

'How do you know it's Eid?' I asked, my mind as usual occupied with night-marches and border vigils rather than festivals and celebrations.

'You forget that I am the signaler,' Kutty beamed, 'I'm in touch with the base.'

As the signaler, he was also much in demand for relaying personal messages whenever the situation allowed him, and was the source of much gossip. In future, I decided, I'd keep my eyes and ears open around him.

For now, Kutty wanted to know if I would say the Eid prayers, and I quickly acquiesced. But Kutty had one request. He had observed that Bullet was never far from me, but for the duration of the prayers, he insisted, the dog needed to be kept away from us.

I was in a quandary. Bullet was not used to being leashed and there was no telling how he would behave if he was tethered now. It would be best, I explained to Kutty, to say our prayers when he was visiting the troops. This meant that we might not be able to say our prayers at the designated time, but I explained that Allah was merciful and would understand, and that it was more important in His eyes that we should say our prayers at all, rather than *when* we said them. Kutty, I was glad to notice, did not voice any objections.

So it was that when Bullet, tail wagging, loped off to inspect the platoon and allow them to pet and talk to him, Kutty and I rolled out our ground sheets, with which bivouacs are made, as substitute prayer mats. I led the prayers and, as is convention, Kutty stood behind me. The prayers offered during Eid are different from prayers recited every day, but I had little knowledge of the specifics, and so with every good intention and to the best of my ability, I offered to Allah what little I knew.

Sometime during the ritual, Bullet returned from his rounds to be greeted by a strange scene. He could make out two people standing in close proximity, apart from the others, muttering something that must have sounded peculiar to his ears. It aroused his curiosity sufficiently for him to come close, but having figured out that it seemed to be a matter of some seriousness, and that it excluded him, Bullet backed off (I could hear Kutty exhale!) and sat down at some distance. He was still observing us but in a detached sort of way. He might not be pious himself, but he knew how to respect piousness when he sensed it.

As the time to return from Hanker drew close at the end of six months, I could not pretend that I was going to miss the picket. The view was spectacular, but it was cold and wet and cut off from civilization, and I was young and the attractions of a town would not come amiss.

What troubled me was the thought of Bullet, who in all the comings and goings of platoons had come to regard me as a constant, the one fixture that bolstered his relationships with the changing faces at the picket. Now he would have to re-establish acquaintance with another post commander.

If it were not for fatigue following the day-long march, I would not have slept at all the first night after I left Hanker. I can still remember the mournful look with which Bullet saw me off the post. Leaving Bullet, and Hanker, caused a greater wrench and sense of loss than I had thought possible.

Over the next two-and-a-half years I was able to put Bullet behind me. I was posted to Kanpur, cantonment life was orderly, and soon settled into a comfortable rhythm of office, football, hockey and volleyball matches, and mess parties. It was good to be young and alive.

Kanpur Club was at the heart of social life in the town and memberships were eagerly sought but not easy to obtain. Fortunately, the Commanding Officer was happy to nurture the high spirits of his juniors, and so we found ourselves often at the Club. If getting in had not proved too difficult, winning favour with Fernandes, the bar manager and an institution in his own right, was another matter. I remember the chagrin of having to wait at the bar while he served the senior membership, treating me not so much as an adult as a 'dependant', till I cheekily demanded a small soda and whisky, only to be served with a small whisky and a bottle of soda.

'Really, Fernandes,' I said to him, 'I expected better from an experienced barman like you.'

Fernandes said nothing but served me the reverse order, as I had requested, beginning a camaraderie that would last several years. Over time, we became the thickest of friends, and he wouldn't mind sharing a piece of gossip or slander with us. Our subaltern group also nurtured a huge appetite, and it was not unusual for each of us to order six to eight tandoori chickens at one go. Emboldened one evening, he said he could remember only one other officer who would order a similar amount of food every time he came to the Club. Asked who it was, Fernandes disclosed his name: Ayub Khan, who had gone on to become Pakistan's youngest full general, its commander-in-chief in 1951, and the nation's second president from 1958 to 1969! In the aftermath of the '65 war, the audience did not express any delight at the information.

Those years in Kanpur, from mid-1966 to late 1969, form among the most cherished memories of my army years, for several reasons.

My next posting, to Rishi Dogri picket in Chini Valley in Himachal Pradesh, beat the hell out of Hanker. The enemy here was a more potent and daily force by way of harsh terrain and harsher weather. Banshee winds howled across a desolate and rocky landscape that was earthquake-prone and suffered frequent landslides. A neighbouring picket was commanded by Everest summitteer the late Major (later Brigadier) A.S. Cheema, who was my radio telephony companion.

Rishi Dogri was perched at a height of 13,300 feet, and with it came Kaka.

Unlike Bullet, who was *bhutia*, Kaka was a *gaddi* dog that had been given the nickname of the reigning Bollywood superstar, Rajesh Khanna, who had created quite a sensation in the area while shooting the blockbuster film, *Aradhana*, in Shimla. No wonder Kaka, who was like Bullet in all other respects and discharge of duties, carried his attitude about him like a trophy.

In one respect, though, he was unlike Bullet. If he found the discipline lax, he would enforce it the only way he knew how. I was soon to be served evidence of it.

There was a small waterfall at the lower post from where water had to be fetched up to my picket daily. A local porter had been hired to fill a *dhal* (a skin bag used for ferrying water) with fresh water and carry it up, a task he performed by hoisting the *dhal* over his shoulder and up the steep gradient of several hundred steps, bent under its weight.

Kaka was naturally suspicious of civilians and tolerated them with ill-disguised contempt. To his way of thinking, they were lazy and slovenly – and now the water-carrier, who had stopped on an incline to rest his *dhal* and back against a curve in the mountainside while he lit his pipe and sucked a few greedy puffs, was offering him confirmation of it.

In remote mountains, far from any habitation, patrol teams are trained to search for smoke and fire as a sign of the enemy's presence. The strictest vigil is maintained to ensure that such giveaways are not permitted. And here was a civilian (naturally!) breaching the rule. Kaka, who needed a mere excuse, launched himself at the poor water-carrier, grabbing him by a fleshy chunk of his thigh and held him prisoner till the poor man's shouts for help resulted in his freedom. But Kaka had taught him a lesson he would not forget in a hurry.

My life in the army might have continued apace, except that long tenures in high altitude locations had affected my health. It was at this time that my wife, Sukhi, and I moved to Poona, an idyllic cantonment town in the Western Ghats. There was a cardio-thoracic centre in the vicinity that I required for my treatment, the climate was salubrious, the army had been kind enough to allot me a bungalow, and all I needed was – a dog!

The realization hit me out of the blue. I liked dogs. No, I loved dogs. Yet, I had never had a dog of my own. It was time to get myself a dog.

A dog did not take long to materialize. My hunt was rewarded somewhat unexpectedly, though rewarded, in hindsight, might not be quite the right term.

Like most pet-owners, what I had in mind when I started out was a puppy. A family that was moving out of station was finding it difficult to take their Labrador with them – did I want it? He was well brought up, of a handsome size (and good-looking in the goofy way that Labradors tend to be) with a fine head and paws. His black coat shone with love and care, and though he was about six years old, I agreed to relieve them of the care of Rocco and adopt him as my own.

It was a decision I would come to regret.

When the family moved, Rocco was given a farewell

consisting of many hugs and kisses and not a few tears, and transferred to our household. We didn't know it then, but life as we knew it was about to change.

When at first Rocco refused to eat, I wasn't perturbed: he was probably feeling abandoned. I enticed him with biscuits; he sulked. I waved bones his way; he turned his handsome head away. I dragged him towards his bowl of food; he growled. I was sure he would settle down, but Rocco's temper only got worse. He became moody and snappy and utterly unpredictable. Clearly, his trauma was far greater than what any of us had been prepared for.

If Rocco was rebelling, Sukhi was putting up an obstinate front. As someone who was both petite and timid, she had been put out by Rocco's size. Having a huge hulk in the house unnerved her. While she could hardly ignore him, she refrained from holding out an olive branch to the distressed creature.

'I'll mind my own business if he minds his,' she said resolutely, and was true to her word.

It wasn't what the vet had prescribed as treatment for poor Rocco. According to him, what Rocco needed was to form close attachments again, which in turn would require a great deal of time and affection.

As the days passed, Rocco's transformation from a well-behaved dog to an ill-tempered brute came as a shock even to me. He didn't eat from his bowl but would snatch food from the table. When he was annoyed, which seemed to be all the time, he'd chew anything he could get his teeth into, just like a spoilt puppy – only, he had a fiercer temper, sharper teeth and a more powerful jaw. He'd refuse to go for walks, then relieve himself in the house, causing Sukhi even more grief. A chasm had now developed and I was trapped in its middle.

Sukhi would order Alok, the servant, to take him out, but

Rocco would refuse to be chastened. If Alok managed to drag him out of the house, Rocco would spite him by marching right back to soil the carpet, leaving Sukhi madder than before. If this was a tug of war, it was clear that Rocco was winning.

Two months had passed and there had been no improvement in Rocco's behaviour. In all of this, Alok had remained impervious to our moods and fights, though it was he who ended up cleaning after Rocco's excesses. For Alok, a dog was, well, a dog, nothing you wanted to get your knickers in a twist over. One day, as usual, he tugged at Rocco's leash when the dog resisted his attempts to be taken out for his constitutional. Maybe Rocco had had enough, maybe Alok was too insistent, whatever the case, Alok soon learned his lesson. Rocco lunged at the hand in which he was holding the leash and tore at his forearm. Rocco's temper would cost Alok a gash of eight inches that required twenty stitches to close.

It also marked the end of Rocco's short-lived but remarkable stay in our house.

I had been in office when this latest episode played out. Alok was dispatched to the hospital to have his wound tended to, and came back determined to punish the dog. Sukhi, who must have been bewildered by the attack, proved to have a steely determination I wouldn't come up too often against. Today was one of those days.

'It's either him or me.' Her tone brooked no nonsense when I got home and the episode was dramatically unfolded for me, Alok's hand alone shutting me up. I might be my own master outside the house, but at home, that day, I deferred to the leader.

'I'll find a solution to the problem,' I conceded miserably.

It turned out, I didn't have to do that either. Moving swiftly, Sukhi had set up Rocco's rehabilitation programme at a farm where friends of ours had been searching for a guard dog. Rocco with his fierce temper would be ideal for the task, though Sukhi had taken the caution to avoid mentioning the attack on the servant. If she could, she would not have waited till the evening before he was dispatched, but I was allowed no choice in the matter. Never before had I seen Sukhi's eyes so flinty. So, much to my chagrin, I acquiesced to the plan. Not once did Rocco look back as he was driven away.

Still, I mourned his loss. He might have behaved badly but at least he had reason to, having been uprooted from a loving family and settled life. I was sure that in time he would have come around to loving us. But all that was now speculation. Even though we were spared cleaning up soiled carpets, and the house no longer smelled of disinfectant, I missed him. Yet, I could hardly speak to Sukhi about him as she went about pretending there had never been a Rocco there, however briefly. I was sure that her determination to banish even his memory from the house was motivated by the knowledge that if she showed any sign of weakening, I might persuade her to allow him one more chance and bring him back. So, if Sukhi was determined, I resolved too that I would not go to visit Rocco in his new home: that might cause me even more grief than I was silently suffering on my own. I then learnt what it meant to be an abandoned dog. Several decades later, I would weep along with U.S. army dog-handlers in a TV documentary, who had to leave behind their canine faithful in Vietnam on orders from their headquarters in Washington.

There were greater changes that lay immediately ahead. I was now determined not to waste my professional life in the backwaters of the army. Yet, what was I to do? In the 1970s, India was still not part of the global economy, and new jobs were no easy pickings. And the army, while a wonderful institution that allowed great camaraderie between officers, at that time hardly provided training for civil life.

While I worried about these matters, an unforeseen sequence of events would prove to be the greatest catalyst of my career and determine my future. At a party in Pune, probably spurred by the ice-cream on offer as dessert, I had held forth about the ice-creams we would make as children in the leaking, wooden ice-cream machines every household used to have, and which were put to use on weekends to churn out the creamy confections. Commercially manufactured ice-creams then rarely ventured beyond synthetically-flavoured vanilla, strawberry, butterscotch or tutti-fruti, while it was my contention that the best ice-creams needed an infusion of natural ingredients as well as more exotic formulations, like fig, or honeydew melon.

Unknown to me, listening with rapt attention to my monologue was P.L. Lamba, who owned Gaylord's and, along with I.K. Ghai of Kwality's, controlled the largest chunk of the branded ice-cream market in India. By a curious coincidence, he was setting up an ambitious plant for making ice-cream in Poona and on only a cursory introduction and a whim, offered me the job of heading the unit. It was scarcely something I could comprehend. What did I know about making commercial ice-cream, or running an ice-cream plant, for that matter? Lamba rubbished my apprehensions, and sooner than I had imagined, I had put in my papers ending my career in the army. But what man proposes, Allah disposes…

Halfway through the project, the owners decided that there was little financial merit in setting up a new plant, and that it made sense to expand their existing capacity in Bombay and supply ice-cream through that plant to newer markets. My dream of a civilian career came crashing down.

I found myself out on a limb. There was no way to retract my papers from the army headquarters, my discharge orders had been issued, and suddenly, in my early thirties, feeling vulnerable, I wondered what I would do next. But when one door closes, another opens. Lamba, realizing that he had had a role to play in my leaving the army, offered me what he considered a compromise option: the family had set up a five-star hotel in Aurangabad. Did I wish to join?

If I knew little about ice-cream plants, I knew even less about hotels. This was the early seventies, and luxury hotels were scarce on the ground. I understood hospitality as instinctively as any other Indian, the army had taught me mess etiquette as well as the basics of constructing a menu, or when to serve port and sherry, or post-prandial coffee and liqueur, and I prided myself on being able to ensure and maintain discipline, but this was scarcely sufficient to manage a five-star property, even in distant Aurangabad. Left with few choices, and glad for the leg-up, I agreed to try out a career in hoteliering.

The next four years were spent in Aurangabad as manager-in-residence at the Rama International. As international tourists poured in from around the world to tour the ancient caves of Ajanta and Ellora, I learned the ropes and adapted quickly to my new environment and, to my surprise, found that I was enjoying the experience and making a mark.

My life might have continued uninterrupted but for destiny, which brought the annual convention of hoteliers to Aurangabad and with it, the person who would forever change my professional life.

Ajit Haksar was the charismatic chairman of tobacco major ITC, under whose stewardship the company had diversified into hotels. He was here in person now, staying at Rama International. He was attending the convention but also scouting for properties to consign to ITC's Welcomgroup chain of 'hotels, resorts, palaces and indovilles', and though I didn't know it then, Rama International was his target on that visit.

I conducted him around the hotel and in a conversation about the project, was able to brief him satisfactorily, as well as engage him on what I knew of the industry, and on something I cherished dearly, the food and beverage (F&B) business. Whether it was my knowledge or enthusiasm, I'll never know, but an offer from ITC was one I would have been foolish to turn down. In 1979, I was happy to switch to the corporate but exciting environment that Welcomgroup offered the talented group of hoteliers that Haksar had managed to assemble.

Soon after, I was asked to make a presentation on the Rama International project at the group's flagship hotel, Maurya Sheraton, in New Delhi. Ahead of me were teams that had come from the group's other properties, each of them consisting of the general manager, sales manager, F&B manager, chief engineer, financial controller, and so on, and the charts and presentations appeared more intimidating than informative. Soon enough it was my turn, and I was asked to come to the dais with my team – which was non-existent, I was the hotel's lone representative at the conference – but which I more than adequately made up for by answering every query that was hurled at me. I knew sufficiently about the project, and I could sense that Haksar was enjoying everyone's discomfort at the extent of my knowledge by putting to me several questions that were not strictly necessary or required.

Following my debut, so to say, with ITC's top management, I was packed off to Kathmandu where a hotel tie-up was giving the company more grief than joy. Nothing much came of the

Kathmandu hotel, and eventually ITC gave up on it, even though the Nepalese capital at the time was a great draw for Indian tourists. I was asked to report to the Maurya Sheraton, where the general manager, K.K. Malhotra, was being sent overseas for exposure to different aspects of hoteliering. In his absence, I became the hotel's resident manager.

If those were some of the most exciting years of my career and life, it was at my next posting in Agra that I would resume my tryst with dogs. Only, by a quirk of fate, this time I would do it professionally.

Though I would not have admitted it then, almost the first thought that struck me as the car curved up to the Aga Khan architectural award-winning hotel in Agra was that it would provide a lovely home for dogs.

Welcomgroup's Mughal Sheraton was a hotelier's delight. At the time, it was probably India's most luxurious resort. From most of the rooms that faced the Taj Mahal, and from its first floor terrace where a telescope had been provided for the purpose, tourists would spend hours looking at the ethereal monument. A huge chandelier hung over the lobby. Specialty restaurants served cuisine that was impossible to find outside the metros. Meandering corridors led to rooms set amidst large gardens spread over a thirty-acre estate.

Once again it struck me – dogs could be happy here. Was I, I couldn't help wondering, becoming obsessive?

Unlike the West, hotels in India are rarely dog-friendly. Even though there is no aggressive lobby against them, Indian guests, in particular, would be uncomfortable at the thought of sharing the premises, leave alone the restaurants, with dogs. But what if

I were to breed them and turn the kennels into an attraction for visitors, as well as a lucrative stream of revenue for the property? Surely there would be no scope for antipathy then.

As I settled into my role as general manager, that idea of housing India's best kennels took root. I had already introduced some changes that had gone down well with the management. One of these was a barbeque restaurant in the garden where guests could, if they chose, rustle up a meal for themselves and their family or friends, from an array of meats, vegetables and condiments laid out like a buffet. Or, if they didn't want to fuss over a stove, they could instruct the chefs present to customize their meal. It had been a success even though, as a concept, it was ahead of its time. Emboldened, I pressed on with my plans to set up the country's premier breeding kennel club at the Mughal, fingers crossed, prepared but not expecting the management to scuttle my plans. Fortunately for me, Y. C. Deveshwar was at the head of the division.

The infrastructure was easy enough to create. There was staff at hand, especially in the lean season when virtually all business shut down on account of dormant tourism activity – the success of summer packages would follow some years later. The only complicated thing to do was to get the dogs in place. I sent letters and people to kennel clubs around the country and soon had a manger of German Shepherds, Dalmatians, Golden Retrievers and Dobermans. Trainers would take them for walks, groom them and make sure they were provided a nutritious diet from the kitchen. Curious tourists wanted to visit the kennels; a marketing programme for breeding and mating packages had been created, and everything was just beginning to take off when I was served my marching orders. As the company's regional director (south), I was briefly based in Madras before being recalled to New Delhi and the Maurya Sheraton.

Had I been given a little more time, I can vouch that the Mughal kennels would have fulfilled their destiny. Abandoned mid-stream, and with no one to take the baton forward, the kennel club ran its course and, over the years, came apart due to lack of attention. I daresay there would be few people today who might even remember the joyful bark of pedigreed dogs in the gardens of the Mughal Sheraton.

If the return to the Maurya Sheraton as its general manager and regional director (north) came with a great load of responsibility, it also came with an added pleasure. The hotel now had an official mascot in the shape of a huge and lovable St Bernard.

Bernie had been my predecessor Anil Channa's idea. I little knew or cared how he'd managed to install a house-dog in Welcomgroup's flagship property, only that the friendly mascot was marched into the property every morning and evening and was warmly received by guests.

Delhi residents who loved dogs chose the Maurya's restaurants for meals so they could meet Bernie. Down in the basement, where she had her home, Bernie was fed the choicest five-star scraps. It was the sort of dog's life that people can only dream about. In due course, Bernie was mated, and the arrival of Bertie was announced in the hotel's newsletter. Mother and son would proudly be paraded on request, and I personally vouch that they greatly enhanced the appeal of the hotel for many visitors.

Greatly though I enjoyed my exchanges with Bernie and Bertie, I remained conscious of the fact that they weren't my dogs but belonged to everybody at the Maurya – the staff and the guests equally.

I wanted my own, exclusive pet and, under cover of the two St. Bernards, I was going to have one. Now that I'd been given a license, I could go ahead with my plan.

Laila was my first-ever pet. She was a German Shepherd and came with a lineage as long as an arm. Even as a pup, she was quite majestic with her double coat and fine features. And she quickly became the love of my life.

As general manager, I had a suite of rooms on the sixth floor, and tempted as I was to keep Laila with me, I knew that it wouldn't look too good. As it is, as the general manager's pet, Laila was spoilt. She was petted more than was good for her, fed the choicest tidbits by the food and beverage team, and surrounded by a ring of affectionate staff members who doted on her. Man Bahadur, who was devoted to Bernie and Bertie and given their charge, now also looked after Laila.

If Laila was easy to love because of the affection she exuded, I had to be careful about how she spent time with me. During the day, she shared her kennels with Bernie and Bertie in the basement of the hotel. It was only in the evenings, or oftentimes nights, when I returned to the suite, that Laila would be sent for. There was no question of her being allowed to use the guest lifts or the staircase, so she'd be guided through the hotel's back door and through the labyrinthine room service corridors up six floors to my suite where, while Sukhi retreated into the bedroom – she had not yet forgiven me for Rocco – I played with Laila.

Often, I'd have a special treat for Laila; or, if we were stepping out for a party, I'd let her snooze in the room while I had a cup of coffee, or showered and changed. In spite of the little time I gave her, Laila lavished me with love. When it was time to send her off every night, she went without a fuss.

Because of the convenience of the staff, and because she visited our suite almost by appointment, I'd had no role in bringing up Laila. She'd been house-trained and looked after by others for the fourteen months that she had made Maurya Sheraton her home.

When I was transferred to the Welcomgroup headquarters as vice-president (operations), it meant shifting out of the hotel. The office found me a bungalow in Greater Kailash I, and after several years of living in hotels, we moved into a home again.

Living in a hotel has its conveniences, but also its restrictions. The joys of room service and endless menu cards soon pale. You can do almost nothing without being observed. The freedom, therefore, of being in our own house was a welcome change for us, though it was clear that Laila missed the pampering, not just of the hotel's staff but, chiefly, of the kitchen's food and beverage team. Yet, the scales must have weighed in favour of our being able to spend more time together. She accompanied me on my morning walks, slept inside the house, was fed delights from the dining table, and had soon inserted herself into every facet of our life.

Sukhi may not have loved her as much, but in her gentle, quiet way, accepted my need for a pet and ensured that Laila was fed and sent to the vet for regular shots and de-worming. She had not yet forgotten the horrors that Rocco had visited on our household and treated Laila with diffidence.

Laila, meanwhile, flowered, became frolicsome, and seemed not to be aware of her own exuberant energy. And so it was that one day, Sukhi came home to be greeted by Laila in her awkward, adolescent fashion. She had grown to a magnificent size, and when she came rushing to greet Sukhi and pounced on her, as was her manner, Sukhi could not retain her balance and fell. Barely avoiding a head injury, she was badly shaken. Once again, it seemed to her like a replay of the Poona incident, only this time, instead of Alok, she had become the unintended victim.

When I returned from office, I was faced with a familiar choice. 'Either she goes, or I go.' Sukhi was inconsolable but intractable. It wasn't a fair choice, and Sukhi probably knew it, which is why she presented me with the solution. I had created the kennels in Agra; Laila would be happy there and I would have additional reason to visit the property that was part of my overall job.

I might have choked back a surreptitious tear, I hardly remember now, though I probably sulked when Laila was packed off. I'd like to think she was happy again in familiar hotel surroundings, in the company of other dogs, allowed to run across the virtually unrestricted spaces and large grounds that the Mughal provided her. Whenever I went to pat her on my visits to the hotel, I could not help sense that though she was comfortable, there was something missing in her life. Did she miss my company, or crave for our life together in Delhi?

At any rate, another phase of my life was over. As managing director of ITC Hotels, I too would soon be moving into a larger house in Panchsheel Park. Sukhi and I had arrived at an uneasy truce. What remained unsaid between us was something that lay at the top of our minds.

Did a larger house mean the arrival of the next big dog in our lives?

Gori Comes Home

Panchsheel Park's N Block is a leafy arcadia without the parking congestion so common in even the toniest of south Delhi's residential colonies. Finding a house here, spread over 1,200 square yards, was a dream come true. The distance from Greater Kailash I may not have been too great – it was within walking distance, though the capital is hardly an ideal city to walk in – but in its mindset, it might have been a different city, or even country altogether. For the better part, residents here kept to themselves and were mindful of each other's privacy. The bungalows were large and set within gardens, providing an oasis from the colony's other blocks and the traffic on the crowded Ring Road close by.

Sukhi should have been happy that my career had taken the course to the very top as the first managing director of ITC Hotels, and with our shifting into a much larger house, but I couldn't shrug off the feeling that she seemed at least a little apprehensive about the change. At first I thought the idea of packing and moving was the reason for her anxiety, though we'd already engaged a packing and moving firm for the actual movement. Or, I might have thought, Sukhi was probably concerned about Shagun. Shagun was Sukhi's grand-daughter, her daughter Chandan's daughter, who came to stay with us in 1995.

Shagun had been studying in the distant Nilgiris, at the residential Lawrence School, Lovedale, near Ooty. Until Chandan decided that she would be better off studying in Delhi for the crucial classes eleven and twelve. As her grandmother, Sukhi could have been stressed about doing a good job of it. Certainly I had taken to her. Shagun was personable without being imposing, and I was glad to play the role of her guardian and step-grandfather.

In all the time Sukhi was setting up the house at Panchsheel Park, I was caught up with changes at work that were cataclysmic and far-reaching. The company itself was moulting into a new entity and I was at its helm, so any spare time was spent in meetings and discussing strategies, often at the cost of meals – some skipped altogether, others rudimentary and basic. At home, the cartons slowly disappeared, shelves were filled with books and objets d'art, our comprehensive collection of art now adorned the walls, dust covers were finally taken off sofas, and carpets were unrolled across floors.

I noticed the changes peripherally, contributing to them as and when I could, and Sukhi seemed to manage quite well on her own. But her eyes remained worried.

On 14 August, I found out why.

It was, as was usual in those days, late by the time I arrived home. I was exhausted and wanted nothing more than a scotch and soda before taking a shower and sitting down to dinner. Unusually for her, Sukhi seemed both boisterous and nervous, and the reason was soon apparent.

As I flung off my tie and jacket, I thought I heard a scratching sound followed by a whimper. It sounded like there was a small creature in the vicinity. Was it a dog in the back lane? I concentrated, but there were no more sounds.

'I have a surprise for you,' Sukhi said.

Instantly, I knew it was a pup. Now I realized I'd walked past a basket, lying in the room leading to our bedroom, without bothering to see what was inside.

'A surprise,' I echoed her, walking into the middle room.

Beside her, snuggling in the basket, was a small bundle of white fur.

My hopes soared.

Did I want tea, or whisky?

I was too excited to answer.

'Now that we have this beautiful, large house,' Sukhi beamed, 'I thought we should bring home a pup.'

'A very small pup,' I pointed out. I had never considered myself knowledgeable about dogs, but if this pup was six to eight weeks old, before which it isn't safe to separate them from their mother, then it was clear this was never going to be a big dog. I had never thought of myself as a purist, but for some reason I seemed to have developed a disinterest, if not a dislike, in small breeds.

'A lovely pup,' Sukhi remonstrated.

'But little, nevertheless,' I argued, unable to help myself. If this was a conciliatory gesture on her part, Sukhi seemed to have muddled up. This wasn't a Labrador or a German Shepherd, it was some small, squeaky, loathsome breed.

'She's so white, and cute, and cuddly,' Shagun joined forces with her grandmother.

I knew I'd been checkmated. Even though I'd been busy, part of my mind was aware that the large garden behind the house was ideal for keeping dogs, and at times my mind had wandered, wondering about the breed of dog I could safely bring home without inviting Sukhi's wrath. But clearly, Sukhi had been better, and faster, at reading my mind and acting on it. Before I brought home some huge monster – I'm sure she imagined a Rottweiler tearing her up – she'd pre-empted the move by scouring her network of friends and contacts to locate a small breed and without being too choosy, had brought home the first little pup she could lay her hands on.

'I think,' Sukhi beseeched, 'you'll love her.'

I didn't feel like a drink any more. I didn't feel like dinner either.

'I know,' I said to Sukhi, 'I'm going to hate her.'

In truth, I didn't much care for the new addition to the household. Besides, I was too involved at work to care. Sukhi and the pup tried to ingratiate themselves into my ambit, but I dismissed them both. I was hurt that Sukhi had been less than choosy when looking for a pet, simply to thwart any desire I may have had to bring home a dog that was larger than the midget she'd smuggled in. I also felt that she neither trusted me, nor thought it fit to discuss with me something as important as a living, breathing addition to our house.

In hindsight, I can see that it was I who was to blame. In the snatches of conversations we'd managed to exchange in the preceding months, I had pointed out the new house's suitability for bringing up dogs. Did I ever think of the terror she had been put through, first with Rocco, and later with Laila? Had I discussed their arrival with Sukhi? I could hardly have expected to be allowed dogs, so the pup was Sukhi's peace offering, the signal of a truce, and a solution to our widely disparate views regarding the ideal pet to have at home.

At the time I was simply hurt. I could hardly bear talking about the pup, but I had to get to the bottom of the mystery.

Where had Sukhi got it from?

Sukhi was uncharacteristically vague. Of course, she realized that if she disclosed her source, I'd probably ask Gopal, the driver, to put the pup in a basket and send her back with a note explaining that there had been a horrible mistake.

What was the pup's breed?

'It's very good,' Sukhi assured me, though she was lying again. As it turned out, the pup was a Spitz, but possibly with a corrupted Samoyed and Pomeranian bloodline.

To prevent any attempt to return the pup, Sukhi cooked up an impossible-sounding story and embellished it with details at the slightest opportunity, usually when the pup came to where I was having breakfast, wagging her tail.

'Her mother died while giving birth to her,' she said emotionally.

Refusing to acknowledge the pup's presence, I said, 'Its mother's owner should keep it as a reminder of the pet.'

Sukhi wasn't easily stymied and her story was laced with increasing melodrama. 'She's going away from Delhi,' she said theatrically. 'The poor pup has no one but us to call her own.'

For once in my life, I was flummoxed. Even though I liked dogs instinctively, I could not imagine some rat-like being usurping the space where I had imagined a gamboling German Shepherd. Could I now openly declare war and tell Sukhi that since she'd got a small breed without my permission, I would now go ahead and get a dog of my choice?

Meanwhile, cruelly perhaps, I'd made sure the pup was not allowed into our room. Her basket remained in the middle room, where she'd crawl around on her fat little tummy, occasionally whimpering, a vexatious presence, though I refused to let Sukhi see I was plotting her departure.

Either the pup would stay, or I, and I wasn't going anywhere in a hurry.

Meanwhile, I thought, I could do without the creature getting underfoot.

'Take her and her basket to the guard-room,' I ordered Vishnu, our general factotum who ran errands at home. 'Tell the guard she's not to be allowed into the house.'

Sukhi, understandably, didn't say anything.

I'd won the battle but now I had to win the war.

Meanwhile, things at work couldn't have been more hectic. The changes that coincided with my leadership of the company's hotel division were complicated, to say the least. But to understand the true breadth of the difficulties, it is important to get a sense of its history.

The decision to diversify beyond tobacco and augment foreign exchange earnings and establish new businesses had been taken under the stewardship of ITC's chairman, A.N. Haksar, in the early 1970s. This was in the days of the 'licence raj', when the state stifled rather than encouraged new businesses. Both the planned diversifications were capital intensive – paper (which would substitute its costly import), and hotels (which would bolster foreign exchange earnings) – and were happening at a time when government laws were oppressive, to say the least.

Haksar retired in 1982 and J.N. Sapru stepped into his shoes to steer ITC's fortunes. Unlike Haksar, Sapru saw little merit in the hotel industry and was less than enamoured of it. His way of thinking was more akin to that of the principal, British American Tobacco, or BAT, which preferred to stay with the core business.

In the short duration that Welcomgroup had entered the fray with its first hotel in Chennai, followed by subsequent additions in Agra, New Delhi and Bangalore, and assorted managed hotels, the hospitality business was already in a churn. The Taj and Oberoi groups, spurred by ITC's foray, had both announced huge investments and were extending their reach, making the market extremely competitive. And Welcomgroup's mix of owned, managed, franchised, and heritage hotels was proving a huge strain – not to say drain – on the company.

It was during Sapru's rein that Y.C. Deveshwar, in 1984, took over as head of the hotels division and was co-opted on to ITC's board of directors at the young age of thirty-six. His first task was to manage the choppy waters of the division with some excellent rearguard action. To his credit, he showed a remarkable talent for the job and though Welcomgroup saw several radical changes, not all of which found favour with senior members at the board, he put the chain on a sound footing. Together we formed a team that would find its mettle tested on several occasions, but would also reap rich rewards.

While I was inducted to the headquarters of the hotels division in August 1990, in May 1991 Deveshwar found a higher calling at the headquarters of ITC Ltd. in Calcutta. The same year saw two significant developments. In the first, Deveshwar was invited by the Minister for Civil Aviation, Madhavrao Scindia, to take over as chairman and managing director of the ailing national carrier, Air India, a bold move on his part. The airline had been under severe pressure from other international carriers and was bleeding revenues. A turnaround was urgently required and Deveshwar was able to provide a degree of resuscitation, at least for a while. The same year saw Sapru retire from the top job at ITC Ltd., to be replaced by K.L. Chugh.

The changes might have settled into place but for a tragic

occurrence in Bombay, where the Welcomgroup-managed iconic SeaRock Hotel fell victim to a bomb blast in March 1993. Though there were no fatalities, the detonation caused a shift in the alignment of the lift well, rendering the hotel unusable for all purposes. I struggled to ensure that at least the restaurants on the ground floor remained operational, and some guests didn't mind staying on the first floor – certainly, as Welcomgroup hands ourselves, that is where all of us stayed on visits to that city – but keeping the hotel operational while insurance, repair, renovation and reopening issues were sorted out with the owners, added to the pressures on the division's well-being and growth plans.

We were in a hurry but were getting nowhere. And the only beneficiary of the tragic circumstances appeared to be the newly-opened Leela, which benefitted hugely from a closed SeaRock.

At this point, Deveshwar was recalled by ITC in February 1994. The company felt it needed him more than Air India did, and he returned as vice-chairman to assist Chugh at a time when its differences with BAT, which was trying to acquire a higher stake in ITC, were out in the open and the increasingly dirty war was being played out in the media. Among the many resolutions at the point, the one that impacted me the most was the decision to hive off the hotels division as a separate company.

Was I the company's hatchet-man brought in to perform an amputation? At no point, though, did I think ITC was playing a game of double jeopardy, but my own colleagues at the time could be excused for thinking that I had been made the fall guy who would decide or destroy their future. The pressure was immense, morale somewhat low, gossip fired the corridors of the hotels, and I could not help sense that everyone was wondering, and whispering, about the course of events behind my back.

On 22 March 1994, events came to a head. I was 'advised' that I should obtain the resignations of the entire staff on ITC

Welcomgroup's rolls, and simultaneously issue them fresh appointment letters on the rolls of the newly-formed company, ITC Hotels, by 31 March 1994. The new entity would come into being on 1 April 1994.

I was aware of the enormity of the task before me. ITC had an eighty-four-year-old history in the country and was known for its corporate culture, which drew some of the finest talent to work within its hallowed chambers. How would colleagues and staff feel about signing out of that company, on to another ITC subsidiary, true, but one with no history at all? What if it was all some giant hoax, a charade?

My biggest challenge, I knew, would be to retain every valued member of the hotels division, and the only way to do it was to meet them personally and assure them, instead of sending them an officious note from the company's headquarters in Delhi, which was liable to be misinterpreted. In that short time, I accumulated more frequent flyer miles than I knew what to do with, as I crisscrossed the country, going from one Welcomgroup hotel location to another. At each location, my first meeting was always with the union leaders, followed by an interaction with the staff. At each location, almost invariably the first question addressed to me would be about my own plans. 'Sir,' a hand would pop up, 'what about you? Are you coming with us or staying with ITC?' At each location, I assured them that I would be their managing director *in the new company*.

In the end, it was all smoothly managed. On D-day, at each hotel, the human resources teams set up queues with two rows of tables on either side. As each employee stepped up, he first signed his resignation letter on the left side, then accepted his appointment letter on the right side. In almost a snap, it was over. I'd pulled off one of the most fraught changeovers without hitch or controversy. In the history of Indian business, it would serve as an example of a flawless transition. Nor could I claim it as my exclusive achievement, for it spoke of the employees' trust in the company and the integrity of its leadership.

Having got the transition out of the way, it was still a task to manage the newly formed company. I was probably a more familiar face in aircraft cabins than in my own office. There were local compliance issues, endless amounts of paperwork, the task of managing everyone's hopes and expectations, and just ahead, a public offer.

It was during this fraught period that the pup had been brought home by Sukhi. Having banished her to the guard's cabin, she was off my radar for the critical days when I was grappling with the exigencies at work.

Yet, I never lost sight of my goal.

I would deal with her before she became a familiar presence and stayed on as a result of my neglect.

The next time I became aware of the pup was in the form of a scrap of paper with a name on it. 'Gauri'.

During her stay so far, I'd not let anyone name the pup, aware of the entanglements of affection that result from such an anointment. I might have lacked decisiveness when it came to deciding her fate – after all, I could hardly throw her out, so would have to play my cards carefully – but it was on account of my frequent travels rather than any relationship that might have been developing with the creature. I'd see her snub-nosed snout peering through the open door of the guard-room when I'd return from office or from my frequent outstation visits, but never once did she venture out, nor once did I call out to her, or give her a pat on the head.

In hindsight, it was behaviour I would come to deeply regret. And in the years to come, it would take extraordinary measures on my part to make amends with her for ill-treating her in those early months of her life.

It is now obvious that soon after she'd been brought home, Sukhi had taken her to the vet for her distemper shots, returning in due course for follow-up jabs. And here was proof of the perfidy.

'Gauri?' I couldn't help but protest.

'She had to have a name,' Sukhi spoke with her back to me. 'The vet asked.'

'But…Gauri?'

'Gori, actually,' Sukhi corrected me.

'But it says Gauri on this form,' I pointed out to her.

'He must have spelled it wrong.'

'But Gauri is a goddess,' I insisted, 'you can't have her being called or spelled that.' I was talking to Sukhi's stiff back.

She shrugged.

I now vaguely registered sibilantly whispered references to Gori/Gauri. It was clear the pup had been christened even before she went to the vet, which the household had hidden from me. What else, I wondered, were they hiding? Had they ganged up against me?

I was all the more determined to be rid of the pup. But before she could be dispatched elsewhere, I resolved to have her name sorted out.

Next morning, I took Sukhi aside. 'Look, she can't be named Gauri. It's wrong. You'll have to get the vet to change the documents.'

'It's only a spelling,' Sukhi pointed out logically, 'it's not as though we're calling her Gauri.'

'It's the principle of the thing,' I said in my *fauji* way, which I knew to a fault saw things only in black and white.

'Okay, okay,' Sukhi acquiesced. I should have suspected that to keep the pup around, Sukhi and the staff would agree to anything, but as usual I was too preoccupied to think that things were other than how they appeared.

That evening, I was back earlier than usual, and found the pup, instead of cowering in the guard's cabin, chasing a ball in the driveway, yapping excitedly, her tail whipping up a storm. For once, even my presence didn't send her cringing away. I couldn't help smile.

Agnes brought in tea. Sukhi, glad to have me home at a civilized hour, was chattering on about mahjong, which she loved with a passion and played with her friends at least a few days every week, and of the other things she had been up to.

'Oh, I went to the vet,' she said.

I paused.

'He was most amused,' Sukhi continued, 'he said now that the Raj was over, I should get over my hangover of white and dark, and that Gauri was a fine Indian name.'

'Not for a dog,' I couldn't help the admonitory note in my voice, 'but why did you think of Gori anyway?' It brought to my mind fair village belles, perhaps because Indian cinema at that time seemed to have more than its fair share of Goris!

'Because she's white,' reasoned Sukhi. 'Anyway, I insisted that she was Gori, not Gauri, and that he should change the name on her certificate.'

I nodded in approval.

'You can't imagine the debate,' Sukhi continued. 'His compounder said Gauri was a better name than Gori, but somebody who had brought a dog to be vaccinated said it could offend Hindu sensibilities, and before I could say anything more, everyone was babbling on about which was the right, or wrong, name. It was like those debates in Parliament where everyone talks at the same time.'

'So what did you do?'

'I seriously thought of changing her name to something like Whisky, or Sherry,' Sukhi looked depressed. I couldn't help smile. In the years I had been in the army, a disproportionately large number of dogs at officers' homes seemed to have had names such as Whisky and Sherry.

'But then the vet asked everyone to quiet down, and I explained to him that you thought it inappropriate, given your religion, that a dog should be named after a Hindu goddess, and that as Indians we needed to be sensitive to such issues.' I couldn't help marveling at how Sukhi, a Sikh, had stood her ground on an issue of religious intolerance that could be used as a stick by unscrupulous people. How commendably she had established her control over something that was morally right.

'And here,' she presented with a flourish a new set of papers with Gori's name, correctly spelt, boldly written on the cover, 'are her credentials.'

I thought of the pup playing in the driveway and resisted a strong urge to send for her.

She now had a name in which I had at least some role to play. I could feel the stirrings of ownership. Had I, by manipulating the change in her name, also changed her destiny?

As I finished my tea, I could sense the pull of an imaginary umbilical cord between myself and the pup – no, Gori, I corrected myself – playing outside. Scolding myself silently for my hyperactive thoughts, I got up to take a shower.

Unknown to me at the time, Shagun had thrown a tantrum of her own.

'What kind of name is Gori?' she'd asked her grandmother.

'It's a nice name,' her Nani stood her ground. 'It's a descriptive name.'

'But Badi Ma,' Shagun tried to convince her, 'it's such a silly, old-fashioned name.'

'I like the name,' Sukhi insisted.

I knew well how headstrong Sukhi could be. But the battle of wills this time was not just between Sukhi and Shagun on account of Gori's name. It was about a much graver issue, that of Gori staying on in our house. And I could be pretty obstinate myself.

In time, we'd figure out whose will and mind would prove the stronger of the two.

By the time August came around that year, the humidity was overwhelming. The air was weighed down by moisture, yet the heat made everything stick to the skin. No sooner had you had a bath, a sheath of sweat covered the body. You couldn't change clothes often enough, and Sukhi grumbled about the heaps of wet laundry because nothing would dry and, after a few days of hanging on the line, would smell like dishwashing rags.

Gori, who still had her home in the guard's cabin, had now worked out my routine. Every time I stepped out for my morning walk, I'd spy her dark eyes peeping hopefully out of the door, as if anticipating when I'd whistle to her to join me. She'd be there when I got into the car to leave for work, and I could swear she'd begun to distinguish the sound of my car from the hundreds that coasted down the road, because her whole body would be wagging a welcome when I drove through the gate – though she always maintained her distance.

I wasn't sure if our situation was irreconcilable, but it seemed the longer she stayed, the better her chances of staying on for good appeared. She was no guard dog, but that's the role I'd cast her in. She was already living in the guard-room. There were times when I could swear her soulful eyes looked at me reproachfully. At those times I convinced myself that I was being fanciful. I was a man of the world doing what I felt was an important job – I couldn't afford to let my attitude soften towards Gori. It isn't as though I'd wanted her, in the first place, or was responsible in any way for bringing her home.

Sometime in the middle of the month, fierce winds heralding the delayed monsoon blew the roof of the guard-room away. Fortunately, no one was hurt, though across the city, tree branches snapped like matchsticks and crashed down on cars, or blew across busy roads to cause traffic-jams. Chaos reigned at home too. Repairs to the roof were required urgently. My landlord felt that as the tenant, it was up to me to undertake these repairs. I thought it was incumbent upon the landlord to manage all such damages. We were both also fond of each other, so what was by no means a large, or even expensive, task dragged on needlessly for over a week.

Meanwhile, the rains, which had begun to pound the city with an intensity that nobody had anticipated, and which resulted in waterlogging in different localities, took its toll on our home too. The guards, bereft of their room, occupied the front verandah. And Gori, robbed of the only shelter she had, found herself home once again.

In any case, I was sure Sukhi had been bringing her in while I was at work. Her easy familiarity with the nooks and corners of the home and her body language suggested a dog that knew her way around the house. Well, I at least wasn't encouraging her to treat the house as her home. There was no choice but to let her sleep in, but she wasn't to be allowed to run around freely.

'Vishnu,' I ordered, 'bring me Gori's leash.'

I chained her to the bedpost in the guest bedroom, both to prevent her from wandering around and also to make sure she did not soil the house. Perhaps because she was used to human presence in the guard-room, or because the rain made her feel cold and uncomfortable, she wouldn't stop whimpering, pawing the floor desperately with her claws, making me wince.

'She's never cried like this before,' Vishnu commented, unconsciously arousing my guilt.

'She'll get used to it,' I said laconically.

Gori continued to scratch and yowl pathetically.

'Bring her into our bedroom,' Sukhi directed Vishnu, gently but firmly.

There was no point protesting – her scraping and howling was keeping me awake in any case. In the warmth of our bedroom, she was immediately quiet, and though she was chained, curled up happily in her basket and went to sleep.

And it was there she slept every night while the landlord and I jousted politely over the responsibility of repairing the guard-room.

Till the night of the storm, that is.

In September, the heavens opened up and descended on the capital in a torrent we hadn't seen in years. It was the kind of downpour that was normal in Kerala, and sometimes in Calcutta or Bombay – but Delhi? Truth be told, I was glad to be home in the evening and not going out anywhere. Lightning streaked across the sullen sky. Thunder set up an orchestra that echoed like a roll of drums before fading out. This was nature not just in peak performance, it was backing it up with all the right props. Raw energy growled as it was unleashed. Fierce wind rattled the doors and windows and howled through the gaps, creating an eerie, moaning sound.

That night, I might even have believed in Unidentified Flying Objects.

That night, Gori wailed even in the comfort of our bedroom. She refused to be quieted by my command, or comforted by Sukhi's soothing murmurs. Pulling at her chain, she struggled to clamber on to our bed, tugging at the comforter with her teeth as she tried to pull it over her head to create a cocoon for herself, all the while whimpering in misery.

That was the night my heart yielded to Gori.

'She won't stop howling till she feels safe,' I said sheepishly to Sukhi. 'I suppose we could let her up for a while.'

I needn't have bothered because Sukhi had already picked her up and brought her to our bed. Gori immediately snuggled under the comforter, next to my legs, where I could feel her trembling. I patted her gently. She licked my hand, and when I withdrew it, she inched up, nestling along my body, till her head rested half on my arm and half on the pillow. I don't know who was more relieved that night, Sukhi or Gori. Certainly, Gori slept soundly, no longer disturbed by the storm, though I could hardly say the same for myself. Mindful of her comfort, I did not change my position the whole night, waking up in the morning with a mild ache throughout my body and a numb arm.

Beginning that night, for all the nights over the next ten years, Gori and I would share a pillow. The little pup had, finally, come home.

Gori's Menagerie

By the following morning, the storm had blown over, though the rain lingered. There was nothing to stop us from tying Gori back to her basket, but she looked up so appealingly, and because I could not find it in my heart to isolate her any longer, she was back for another night of contented sleep, while I lay unmoving and restless. A few more nights and I feared I'd turn into an insomniac, so I decided that Gori would be chained again, this time to the lower bedpost, on a short leash, so she could sleep on the bed but not be able to creep up all the way to my shoulder or the pillow.

I'd love to say that I succeeded in my ploy, for of course I didn't. Clearly unhappy at being 'punished', Gori would struggle throughout the night as she tried to pull the chain all the way to the head of the bed. Now these sounds would keep me awake, or I'd sit up alarmed as she choked in her attempt to break loose. On several occasions I'd return late – whether from office or an official function – to find Sukhi fast asleep, Gori beside her, eager to fight for her right to my pillow. It seemed too much of an effort, and considering I'd relent once in a while, I buckled in and gave way to her wish. A couple of weeks after she'd first set her paws on our bed, Gori made my pillow her permanent and favourite resting perch. From then on, she'd sleep with her head on my shoulder, or on the pillow, else nestled under the sheets, beside my legs.

Soon enough, Gori's life began to revolve around my comings and goings, or so I liked to think. Sukhi, who had been a silent, but giggling, onlooker to our evolving relationship, was probably instrumental in abetting Gori. She must have been glad of my acceptance, finally, of the little pup's place in the hierarchy of the household, for she could not have forgotten the initial motivation that had abetted it. If she relaxed her vigil even a little, who knew what monster I would visit upon her?

'Vishnu, get Gori to see Sahib off,' she'd command in the morning, till it had become a ritual. Gori would patter out to the verandah where she'd wait for a nuzzle from me, and give my face a lick. She was already used to waiting for me to return in the evenings, and I believed she could recognize the sound of the car's engines at some distance. By the time I drove in, she'd be waiting in the verandah, tail wagging, wanting to be picked up for a welcome-home kiss-and-lick.

'I never get that kind of welcome,' Sukhi mock-complained, but I could see she was relieved that Gori and I were becoming inseparable.

By October, I'd started taking Gori with me on my morning walks. She was now four months old and curious as hell.

Ever since I shifted to N-115 Panchsheel Park in 1995, I have gone for walks in the park close to my house. A dusty trail skirts it, passing by Panchsheel's elegant houses and dotted with straggly trees and undergrowth. The park itself, gifted by the city's lieutenant-governor of the time, Jagmohan, is popular not just with those like me looking to exercise but also with children out to play a rough game of cricket or football in the evenings. There are cows, peacocks that come in to find insects from the groves of trees fringing the colony, and quails, snakes, mongooses, jackals and other small animals that inhabit any underbrush typical of north India. Back then, the park was less popular than it is today. Then, one had the liberty of unleashing one's pet and allowing it a free run through the park without fear of causing, or being caused, any injury.

Of course, there was no accounting for the trouble that Gori might get into. She was a pup still, inquisitive, alert, her ears cocked to any new adventure or mischief she could get up to. She was also discovering a world in which other strange creatures lived, and she was keen to make their acquaintance.

Given her size, the animals that first caught her attention were the park's many squirrels. They'd run down trees, skip across the grass, and scamper back up the branches in a manner that fascinated Gori. She'd bark and chase after them, her rump trembling with excitement, full of the accomplishment of victory as she dashed after one, then another, and another. There was no way she could ever catch one, and it provided her with good exercise, so I let her give chase till she was exhausted.

Now that she'd begun to gain in confidence, her next target was any bird that dared to alight on the ground ahead of her. She'd scamper after them, and then bark indignantly when they'd fly away. Crows came next, their black coats lending an easy target as they gathered at a waterhole, or stopped to feed off the stale bread and rotis some walkers left for them at a few chosen spots. Squawking, the crows would lift off and wait for Gori to come back to heel, before returning to finish their meal. Over the next few months, Gori became chuffed with her own importance. Yip-yip-yip, she'd chase after some unfortunate crow or squirrel, and return full of triumph. She was the vanquisher, everyone was terrified of her. She could hardly wait for the next challenge!

That next challenge came by way of creatures much larger than her whom she felt emboldened or honour-bound to take on. These were the peacocks and peahens that descended on the park with their cat-like mewling at day-break. At first they were probably a little scared of Gori – who knows what a pup can get up to in its eagerness – but soon enough learned to tolerate her. Gori would give them chase, and when they'd lift off noisily, she'd turn around to look at me exultantly, as if grinning to say, 'Boss, did you see that?'

'Good girl,' I'd say, beckoning her back. She'd start to trot over, only to be diverted by a darting squirrel or a low-flying peahen, and would be off again. The peacocks were soon on to her tricks. When she'd charge at them, they'd take a short flight and land ahead, waiting for her to catch up again. No sooner was she near they'd perch on a tree branch, or broken wall, while Gori barked in frustration. Then she'd turn around to look at me, as if pleading, 'What do I do now?' It was entertaining to simply watch her, and I suspect I got less walking done than I would have liked to because I had to stop every now and then to summon her over.

As much as she liked her walks in the park, Gori enjoyed rides in the car even more. In those days, I would often insist on driving myself, but Gori wouldn't let me steer without finding a way to crawl into my lap where she would sit squirming, poking her head through the steering wheel, or trying to look out of the window, making a nuisance of herself in any way possible. As a result I'd swerve suddenly, or miss noticing an overtaking car, and was saved some accidents by fortuitous circumstance rather than good driving. The disapproving glances of drivers as they passed me by were enough to sap my morale.

I found a way to prevent Gori from perching on my lap by putting her down on the co-passenger's seat with a cushion to sit on and winding down the window for her to look out and feel the breeze on her face. This might have won us admiring glances – everyone seems to love seeing a dog take a ride in a car – but I soon realized it was more stressful for me. The window had to be lowered sufficiently for her paws and nose to jut out, but it meant minding her constantly in case in her enthusiasm, she leapt out of the car or was hurt by a vehicle driving too close.

It was while she was taking in the breeze that we ended up in what might have been a horrible accident. As we stopped at a traffic signal, a car coasted up beside ours. In its backseat was a lady with a pup in her lap. She too had rolled the window down, and the pup was looking out. The moment Gori set her eyes on the pup, she yapped joyfully and inched forward, wanting a closer look or sniff at one of her own kind. In her excitement, she rushed ahead and her body fell out. I was just about able to catch her by the tail and pull her in, yelping in pain.

For all her troubles and grief, she earned herself a whack from me.

She wasn't going to get any more rides with me, not unless there was a driver to steer the car while I kept an eye and an outstretched hand out for Gori.

If she learned her first lessons of independence in the park, Gori also came up against her nemesis there.

In one corner of the park is a temple. Walkers stop by every morning and evening, and at the vesper hour, the temple bell rings out melodiously. The priest, or someone in his retinue, keeps a cow. When Gori was a pup, the cow had given birth to calves that would suckle their mother, or nibble on the grass laid aside for them. True to their nature, they would trot through the park, playfully butting each other, unaware that Gori, who had watched them teeter and walk and now run with increasing confidence, saw them as a threat to 'her' park. Young as she was, she recognized them as being younger, and so, of little consequence. Off she went after them one day, and they led her along on a merry chase that soon developed into something of a daily routine.

Then Gori did something incredibly stupid. Emboldened by her success with the calves, she charged at their mother, a beautiful cow with well-developed horns. Maybe the cow felt insulted by Gori. Or merely irritated by her yapping, or concerned about her calves. Whatever the reason, instead of ignoring the barking pup, the cow turned on Gori and charged back.

At first, Gori was merely astonished, then bewildered, and finally frightened. With her tail between her legs, she ran panting all the way back to me, though the cow had given up after a short charge. For the first time, Gori had been challenged. She might have remembered the lesson and stayed far off the cow's course, only, the cow wasn't going to allow Gori to forget the lesson she'd learnt in a hurry. Astonished perhaps by the pup's audacious behavior – she was, after all, *gau mata*, whom everyone looked up to, garlanded, gave special treats to on auspicious days – the cow took to charging at Gori every time she spotted her in the park. She'd even hide in the bushes and appear snorting from behind them, startling Gori into flight.

For a while, the cow and Gori had developed into a huge problem for my morning walk. No longer could I relax as I took in my constitutional. Instead, I had to be constantly on guard, always on the lookout. It would be a while before the cow tired of the game, and we could walk again without the bother of a bump in Gori's rump.

Nevertheless I, not Gori, had the scare of my life a few weeks after the threat from the cow had blown over.

I had relaxed my vigil once again, and we'd be out of the house by six in summer and six-thirty in winter, like clockwork. As soon as we got to the park, I'd unleash Gori, and she'd trot ahead while I brought up the rear. She'd chase after squirrels and scare away birds and trot on contentedly, occasionally stopping to sniff whichever bush or shrub caught her fancy.

One morning, as she scampered ten or twelve feet ahead of me as usual, I saw a cobra with its distinctive colour and hood marks slither from one bush to another. Its movement, and perhaps because she had never before seen such a creature, caught Gori's attention. Head cocked, off she sailed to explore the new creature and add it to her treasury of experiences. When I saw her scuttling into the bushes, I screamed, loud and terrified. If she crossed the cobra, there was no way she would live. Maybe because she'd never heard me shout like that before, or because of a primordial sense of danger, she turned back to look at me, giving the cobra enough time to disappear, deeper into the bushes or down some hole. By the time Gori turned back to look, her quarry was gone.

Sensing that it was no longer safe, I decided that Gori should not be allowed to run free. Not only could she become a victim to some other snake, or the outraged cow, but she had occasionally been mauled by stray dogs in the vicinity who saw her as a spoilt, bathed and perfumed dog. Naturally, she was the envy of the bitches, and perhaps caught the eye of the males of the packs that roamed the locality. From now on, Gori would need to be protected.

Gori's adventures with other creatures that God made were not confined to the park. The garden behind the house, with its curtain of trees, provided an uninterrupted passage to birds, squirrels and stray cats that used the territory unmindful of the physical barriers we might have created to separate one house from another and as a deterrent to thieves. Among the denizens that passed regularly through our patch of green was a tomcat that was clearly not young, had experienced the ways of the world and was master of his own destiny. He'd steal stealthily through the garden at night and at times we'd hear him caterwauling noisily and would have to stuff our ears to catch some sleep. In the winters he wasn't above snoozing in the sunlight in the yard, warming his bones as he licked his paws and wiped his face clean.

It was clear that there wasn't much that shook the tomcat's confidence, and Gori certainly wasn't among those that could. Only, Gori didn't yet know her place in the scheme of things. Wired into her DNA was a little chip that told her that she was a dog and dogs chased cats. She may have lost her battle with the cow, but she had taken on calves and peacocks, and they were both bigger than her. Besides, this was her backyard. She wasn't going to stand some smartass cat lording it in her neck of the woods.

So Gori did what she was wired to do. The next time the tomcat came loping through the backyard looking for a tasty scrap, Gori perked up and without as much as a thought, charged at her target.

Instead of turning and fleeing, the cat stood his ground, till Gori was close. This brought Gori up short. Why wasn't her prey fleeing? The cat, meanwhile, resumed its leisurely amble along the wall.

So he's scared after all, Gori probably thought, and was up and giving chase once again. The cat, on its part, was determined to teach the pesky pup a lesson. After all, he came foraging here frequently and didn't need the interruptions of some stupid canine. As Gori charged towards it, the tomcat stopped abruptly and turned to face its quarry.

For Gori, it was literally a split-second decision to apply her brakes and come to a standstill, shocked that the cat was not fleeing. Taking advantage of Gori's surprise, the cat stepped smartly forward, raised a paw and smacked Gori across her face.

That was the last time Gori chased a cat. Thereafter she kept a healthy distance from the families of cats that wandered about the neighbourhood. But she never forgot the insult and humiliation of the tomcat's smack.

Years later she would extract her revenge, but by then she wouldn't be alone.

A Matter of Honour

For all her bravado, Gori was not the bravest little dog that there was. Sharp sounds would startle her. She was not used to arguments at home, which is why street brawls scared her. But nothing frightened her as much as Diwali firecrackers.

Fireworks annoy dogs because their hearing is very acute. They cower for shelter not so much out of fear but because they feel assaulted. Imagine, if you will, being surrounded by high-pitched shrieking and you will have some idea of how the poor creatures feel. It is why even big dogs look as wretched as small ones. Over the years they seem to adjust to the sounds, realizing that terrifying though they are, they will soon pass. Besides, if they don't seem to harm humans – who actually exult in all the smoke and noise – then it's probably not something lethal.

But Gori never outgrew her paranoia of the howls, whistles and explosions of Diwali. Days before the festival, when children down the road began setting off the stray firecracker from their hoard, she would look for the familiar shelter I'd designed for her the first year she came home. And that would become a temporary home till a few days after Diwali, when all the pyrotechnics were exhausted.

That first year, when the firecrackers seemed interminable to her, she'd hidden under my writing table. Since it was shielded by a wall at the back, it must have muffled the noise somewhat. Still, she continued to look uncomfortable, so I placed my briefcase to block the open side of the table, and to augment it further, draped a towel like a tent's flap over the front. It was here she stayed all those evenings when sparklers and explosives were being detonated all around.

Every Diwali, we recreated her sanctuary under the writing table, placing a cushion on the ground for her to sit on. If I delayed creating her soundproof cell, she'd paw on the ground in frustration, as if to say, 'Come on, get with it, why are you dawdling, can't you see it's upsetting me?'

Still, she came to accept Diwali as part of her annual rhythm. What she could not get used to were firecrackers going off at random. There we would be in front of the television, watching India play Pakistan for a test match or a one-day, her master behaving oddly and even shouting madly, when all of a sudden the screen would explode and the neighbourhood would be engulfed with the sounds of celebration – fireworks going off in the sky. Or, there'd be the sound of a screechy band and the blare of horns somewhere in the vicinity, followed, inevitably, by firecrackers. Gori would look towards the desk and then at me. I'd shake my head, and Gori would snuggle deeper under the blankets to blank out the sounds.

These humans, I imagined her brain whirr, they're mad.

Shagun, our granddaughter, would come back home after school to be served lunch at the dining table in the living room. If Sukhi mollycoddled her, I have no shame in admitting I spoiled her, slipping her extra pocket money behind her Nani's back whenever I could, and bringing her gifts from my frequent travels out of Delhi.

Shagun, I know, loved Gori as much as Sukhi and I did, but a part of her also resented the dog.

'You love her more than you love me,' she would frequently accuse Sukhi, and sometimes me as well.

I could well understand why she might feel that way. We'd waited for years, talked about Shagun coming to live with us, done up her room for her, and looked forward to having a young person in the house. And yet, Gori had overtaken the household and our affections. So, though Shagun loved playing with her, tugging at her tail or her ears in jest, every once in a while, she admitted she'd pull just a little harder or longer, when she felt particularly resentful of Gori.

For a few years, it was clear the household ran around the whims of Shagun and the fancies of Gori, or the other way round. 'You spoil her silly,' Shagun would grumble. Gori was bathed and groomed to a fault, her nails impeccably clipped, her coat maintained spotlessly white and perfumed. Of course, we spoiled Shagun silly too, but in a nice, balanced way that wouldn't tolerate any brattishness.

For all their competitiveness, Shagun and Gori might have been umbilically linked.

On the afternoon in question, Shagun came as usual from school and had her lunch supervised by Sukhi. As she got up to walk to her room, she brushed past the curtains, causing a lizard that was hiding there to fall out.

If there's one thing Shagun could never stand, it was lizards. And now her squeamishness took a turn for the worse when she realized she might accidentally have touched the lizard.

'Oh, how she screamed,' Sukhi told me that evening.

'And how Gori barked!' Shagun butted in.

The two had apparently had a slug fest of screaming and barking, each building on the other's hysteria, till even the guard came charging in, expecting the worst.

'I was glad when it was over,' Sukhi confessed. 'Please, will you remember to call the people who do our fumigation? I don't think I can take too much of this kind of excitement.'

Among the security guards on duty was one called Balganand, who was very fond of Gori and enjoyed taking her out on the colony's roads for a short stroll whenever the opportunity offered itself, usually in the late afternoons. Unknown to me, or anyone else at home, he was unwittingly putting Gori's life in danger.

Neighbouring Panchsheel Park, in the shadow of the ancient walls of Siri Fort, is the village of Shahpurjat. Today, a part of it has become an oasis for designers looking for inexpensive accommodation and showrooms, while the rest of the village is home to the workforce that services our neighbourhood – drivers, cooks, maids, peons, blue-collar workers. Those whose homes have been leased by the city's smart-set find themselves with more money than they had ever imagined. Their children, rich without responsibility, drive about rashly in newly-acquired cars, wearing swish clothes and shades, aspiring to the ways of the middle-class.

If Shahpurjat has its share of good samaritans, it is also home to a number of unemployed youth, some of whom, perhaps frustrated by their inability to land a career, hang around with the village's nouveau-riche, unleashing if not a reign of terror then creating enough nuisance in surrounding colonies. The small businesses that had grown in a motley fashion had attracted immigrant labour and ruffians in equal measure.

In 1999, one such group of roughnecks took it upon themselves to terrify Gori.

Perhaps because they drove around aimlessly, the gang would scare poor Gori whenever Balganand took her out for a walk. Out of nowhere, their white Maruti would come careening straight for the duo and screech away just in time to avoid an accident. Emboldened each time, they had started coming nearer and nearer, missing Gori by just a whisker. Balganand would shout after them, but they probably just laughed at him. And I can only imagine Gori being frightened to death by the experiences.

I was informed of the incidents only when their frequency had increased alarmingly and the risk to Gori grown exponentially. Balganand appeared shaken when he reported the matter to me on my arrival back from office one evening.

'Didn't you do anything?' I asked, making an effort to control my temper.

'I made a note of the registration number of the car,' Balganand delivered his testimony, about which I would compliment him later. Just then, I was too upset to think of anything but catching the perpetrator by the scruff of his neck and shaking him till he fell to the ground on his knees to apologize.

'Do you know who they are?' I asked.

No, Balganand didn't, but it didn't take much to fathom that they must live in Shahpurjat.

Nothing could stop me from hoofing it immediately to Shahpurjat, even though it was past eight at night. Once there,

I started searching for the white Maruti, its registration number scribbled on a piece of paper I clutched in my hand. As luck would have it, I spotted the car almost instantly and, further up the lane, a group of young men playing a raucous game of cards.

'Do you know who this car belongs to?' I gestured towards the Maruti.

'Who wants to know?' someone from the group asked.

'I do.'

'On what business?'

'Its owner keeps troubling my dog. Do you know him?'

Loud laughter was followed by sinister silence. I could see a near-empty bottle of whisky that they'd been passing around between them. Clearly, I'd let my feelings, and temper, get the better of me, for this was not a situation I could control.

'A dog,' someone guffawed. 'You're worried about a dog!'

'It's a living being,' I stood my ground. 'Besides, you can't drive rashly on the colony's roads.'

'*Kya tumhare baap ki sadak hai*,' one of them in a flowered pink shirt shouted. 'It's not your father's road. I'll drive how I choose.'

It was an uneven match with several drunkards, and deciding that valour was the better part of discretion, I turned around and marched back the way I'd come, their laughter and curses following me till I was out of their sight.

Round one had gone to the louts.

If there's one thing I loathe, it is using connections to get things done. In a city where everything from a water meter to a fresh passport requires someone to intervene, I'd refused to use my 'contacts' for any mundane task. My reasonably high-profile job meant that I often met and dined with the city's influential gentry. No one could fault me for asking them for favours.

Clearly, the time had come to make an exception to that rule. Arriving home short of breath, I picked up the phone, dialed an acquaintance and presented my case. This was not just a matter of my injured ego, though I cannot deny that it had played a role, but, I justified my action, and said it was a matter of animal rights too. Why should a dog on a leash in a residential enclave feel threatened by some hoodlums? As it is, stray dogs, or cows, are treated with callousness. Perhaps it was time to teach somebody a lesson. Hearing me out, my acquaintance told me to go and rest, that things would take care of themselves.

The next morning, I left for my walk at six-thirty as usual. Returning an hour-and-a-half later, I found a retinue of people gathered at my gate. Among them, I recognized the flowered pink shirt, if not its wearer, though I could see he had teamed his colourful shirt with white trousers and white shoes. Was there fresh trouble in the making?

Standing beside the flowered shirt was an elderly man whose mien spoke of him as being the village elder. Flanking them on either side were two well-built men who I recognized as plainclothesmen. The miscreant, for it was he, joined his hands in a supplicant's gesture.

'I'm really sorry, Sir, I'll never trouble your dog again.'

'You have no right to trouble any dog at all,' I barked, 'or any person, for that matter.'

'You're right, Sir, I'll never trouble anyone ever again,' he pleaded, falling to my feet.

'I apologize on this boy's behalf for any trouble he may have caused you,' the village elder interceded.

'It's alright,' I was quick to accept the act of contrition.

'Apology accepted. Don't do it again. You may go now.'

I could see bewilderment flit across all their faces. Clearly, orders must have gone out at night, and the louts rounded up before the break of dawn, the head of the village summoned, the charges explained, and here they were, expecting a long and drawn out lashing, but finding themselves dismissed.

'Sahib, I'm really sorry,' the scruffy youth continued to plead, expecting the harshest of indictments.

'It's okay,' I said again. 'You made a mistake for which you have apologized, and you can go home now.'

'I hear that you were in the army.' Approval shone in the elderly man's eyes.

I nodded.

'I was in the army too,' he shared.

We chitchatted about the regiments we had served in. The young man looked on nervously, wanting to make amends, but now ignored by everyone as having no consequence.

'Don't do it again,' I turned to him.

He nodded. We'd worked out a compromise in which all was right with the world, and even though they might not have appeared to have lost, it was, I could not help thinking, game, set and match!

My Life with Gori

What they say about mad dogs and Englishmen probably also applied to Gori and me.

On some Saturdays, and usually on all Sundays, I enjoyed waking up later than usual, a break from the crushing routine of office. On such days I would postpone my walk to much later in the day, which would not be much of a problem during winter, but could be thought insane in the middle of summer when temperatures would rise well past forty degrees.

I'd like to blame it on my military training, and even told Sukhi that it was my way of combining exercise with a steam and sauna. But I suspect it was just my way of having a lazy morning followed by a brunch or lunch and then, having prevaricated enough, to finally, even reluctantly, set out, for I might delay the walk but would never avoid it. It was the one thing I tried not to miss when travelling, though it was inevitably difficult, which is why, whenever I was home, weather permitting, I wouldn't miss my walk.

Plenty of people might think that walking in the middle of a summer afternoon is hardly wise. But given my interest in hotel food and beverages, and the too-many occasions when I had to eat out, it was one absolute way of keeping my health and wellbeing in check.

But what was a matter of habit for me became, I know, a cruel indulgence for Gori, for she would insist on accompanying me on my hour-and-a-half-long walk. And so, with temperatures rising to forty-two and even forty-three degrees celsius, we'd set out, the two of us, with all the roads and the park absolutely empty. I'd start my mandatory rounds of the park. From under the leafy shade of trees, I could see the park's staff grinning at the crazy duo, too lazy to come out to bid even the mandatory *salaam*.

I would feel the sweat running down in streams which even the cotton t-shirt could not absorb, and Gori, her tongue hanging out, looked like she would collapse. But valiantly, she would keep up, matching step for step. For a little dog, she not only had a lot of stamina but also a very strong streak of loyalty. Even though these outings exhausted her, never once did she flinch and, indeed, I would have had a more difficult time keeping her back than taking her along.

Back home, I'd rehydrate myself with a solution of Electrol in lime water – something I would have recommended for Gori, but dogs refuse any such beverage. She'd lap up the water from her bowl noisily and then collapse on the floor next to it.

Truly, she must have thought, her master was mad. How was she to know that far from being eccentric, it was behaviour perhaps typical of an ex-infantry major.

Used as she was to my being gone for the day, Gori would start creating a fuss the moment she sensed I was going out for longer.

My frequent travels had trained her well, and from the size of my valises, she could tell how long I'd be gone.

As long as it was the briefcase that accompanied me out of the house, she'd lick me warmly as she bid me goodbye for the day, a ritual she adhered to till her last day. She'd accompany me to the verandah and wait to be lifted so she could get a lick and, when possible, a couple of extra licks of my face. I couldn't help wondering what the society ladies, who sometimes greeted me with a peck on the cheek, would think if they knew who'd got there before them! My return in the evening was a boisterous affair, and I had to spend a couple of moments with Gori before even Sukhi could greet me.

'Badey Pa doesn't speak to any of us for at least a half-hour after he comes home,' Shagun would grumble to her grandmother. How could I explain to her that quieting Gori was not something I could abandon? But I did point out that a half-hour was an exaggeration. 'It's just a few minutes,' I'd say, giving her a hug.

When I packed or took out an overnight case, Gori's send-off was decidedly colder. She could sense I would not return that night, and was somewhat less effusive because of this 'betrayal'. The medium-sized case was truly troubling, for it indicated I would be gone for anything from a few days to a week, and she would find that unsettling. She'd mope, not come out when called, and generally sulk. Yet, she'd bounce out when I was leaving for her farewell kiss. I could never leave without feeling guilty.

The large suitcase was anathema. The moment it was taken down from the attic, Gori would go into a state of depression. That large suitcase meant I was going overseas, whether on a working trip or, more likely, a vacation. She'd calculated by now that it meant my absence from the house for anything between ten days to a month. Even before I'd left, she'd start fussing over her food, sometimes not eating till I'd coaxed her into having a special broth.

Among the help at home, those who looked after Gori were Agnes, Sukhi's maid, the cooks, Javed and Ahmed, the driver, John, and Vishnu, to whom Gori, for some reason, had taken a violent dislike. If Sukhi and I were both travelling, or out in the evenings, Gori would sleep beside the bed in our bedroom, next to Agnes and her young son, if it was for the night or a short trip, and in Agnes' quarters if we were gone from Delhi for longer. She was by now so used to sleeping beside people that there was no way to coax her back into her basket. I could never thank God enough that Agnes had turned out to be a dog-lover and thought nothing about fussing over Gori's increasingly elaborate requirements.

Vishnu, on the other hand, was Gori's bête noire. From a mild-tempered dog, she'd turn snappy whenever it fell to him to take her out for a walk. She'd strain at the leash, which Agnes would have to snap on since Vishnu could attempt the task only at the risk of a sharp nip on his wrist. If he ever entered the bedroom during the day when Sukhi and Gori were resting, she couldn't resist growling at him. I could only imagine Vishnu's crime to be some rough play when Gori had been a resident of the guard-room, for he was an amiable, likeable fellow unlikely to cause offence.

If Gori had set herself up as Sukhi's protector in my absence, she completely ignored her mistress when I was around. I sometimes wondered how Sukhi felt about it. When I was home, Gori would fail to respond to Sukhi's commands.

'Does it bother you?' I once asked Sukhi, for it was she who had not only brought Gori home, but also tended to her when she was a pup.

'Not really,' Sukhi smiled. 'The moment you are gone, she'll transfer her affections to me. I may come second, but I spend more time at home than you do.'

Gori, I realized, was either very selfish, or had learnt how to divide her time and attachments loyally and with complete dedication.

Now I had to find a way to ensure that she did not mope during my long absences away from home. I would often dictate notes or short messages to my office staff while commuting, and it was this that gave me the idea of leaving a series of recorded endearments on a dictaphone for Gori the next time I was going to travel outside Delhi.

'You should have seen her,' Sukhi laughed. 'There was the strangest expression on her face when I played her your messages.' At first she'd been startled. Despite the phonetic distortion caused by the recording, she soon recognized that the voice was mine. 'Sahib,' Agnes giggled, 'she kept wondering where you were, and how your voice was coming out of the dictaphone, sniffing and jerking her head as though she might somehow solve the mystery!'

Pleased that my experiment had been a success, and that I could ease her pain of separation somewhat, I'd ask Sukhi or the servants to put on the speakerphone after my conversation with them, so I could speak to Gori and hear her bark her approval. Soon, the phone became a regular way of staying in touch with Gori when I travelled.

It must have been a year after Gori's arrival in our lives that Sukhi and I were vacationing in Europe. In Prague, the weather was perfect, the skies blue with floating clouds on a day I was hanging out in the city square, a lovely part of the city with inspiring architecture.

For all my interest in food, I'm not a fussy eater, and have no qualms whatsoever about eating the simple fare served at *langars* in gurudwaras with relish, and even street food. Still, it was unusual that I'd bought two hamburgers off a cart, and was munching on one as I took in the sights and the tourists walking around with cameras strung around their necks, taking pictures, laughing, sharing jokes. It was the kind of day that made you thankful to be alive.

Loping along the historic precincts, I saw a hippy strumming a guitar and stopped to listen – would he, as so many did to attract tourists, play the *Blue Danube*, the one tune that everyone both seemed to know and like? The singer was shabbily dressed, his hair appeared matted, and a piece of cloth was spread out before him on which generous tourists had thrown a few coins.

I stayed to listen not because he was particularly good, but because sitting next to him, and looking as disreputable as him, was a battered collie. The poor dog looked maltreated. He was mangy, parts of his coat were missing, an eye was bruised, one ear had collapsed, and when he stood up, I could see he walked with a limp. Instinctively, I could tell that the dog was at the receiving end of the guitar-man's viciousness. There is nothing I abhor more than people mistreating animals, and I felt the blood rush to my face.

Unwrapping the second of my hamburgers, I skipped up the steps towards this motley couple with my hand extended towards them. The hippy, who had been eyeing me, extended his hand to accept the offering, but I was brusque. 'Sorry, mate,' I said to him, 'this one's for your dog.' I had thought he might shower me with abuse, but to his credit the hippy just sniggered. 'You're damn right,' he said. 'He deserves this more than I do.'

While the dog wolfed down the burger, the hippy shared his story with me. He'd been sleeping in a shelter, he said, when an abandoned puppy adopted him. 'He was shivering with cold,' he explained, so he covered the poor little thing with his sleeping bag. That was a year and a half ago, but the dog refused to leave him. It was quite apparent that the hippy was no stranger to hallucinogens, and confessed as much. 'Often, in my stupor, hw said, 'I've kicked and boxed and even starved the blighter, but he won't go away.'

I was moved by this story of two homeless souls providing each other succour, however spartanly. How easily we ignore the mutts on the roads of our cities and rarely give a thought to the street poor who feed and care for them more selflessly than you or I. Patting the dog, I took out a ten-dollar bill and gave it to his reluctant master. 'I hope you'll share it,' I said, 'with your dog.'

I could not help compare the fate of the poor dog with that of Gori. They were roughly the same age, but while one was abandoned and destitute, Gori was the apple of so many people's eye. I shared some of the events of the day when I called home to speak to the servants, but I guess the woof I heard was just Gori reprimanding me that while she was happy to hear my voice, it was time to think of heading back home.

That night, I lay awake for a long time, nagged by guilt for my behaviour with Gori when she was a little pup. Back then, had I been any better than the vagrant with his beat-up dog on the streets of Prague?

Ours was a household that revolved around food, and it was inevitable that Gori would benefit from its spoils.

I cannot say that growing up in Hyderabad, I had any greater or lesser propensity towards fine-dining than any other Hyderabadi. While dining etiquette is a peculiarity of Lucknow, in Hyderabad, too, it is almost instinctive to learn about the right cuts of meat, the tenderizers, condiments and spices that best serve a dish, the accompaniments – it is an entire culture bred around the kitchen and the dining table without fuss or hyperbole.

I must have imbibed and carried these refinements with me, for I was particular about the food served in the mess while I was in the army. Even when patrolling pickets, I would ensure that the men were fed well not just in the sense of plenty, but also quality. It had required innovation on my part, when we had been starved of air-dropped supplies on account of inclement weather, to use whatever was at hand – bamboo shoots, rock salt, perhaps a fresh catch from the many streams in the area – to cook up something that was not just palatable but also nutritious and would ensure the troops' health and immunity.

Once I joined the hospitality trade, with plenty of opportunities to introduce, experiment, and innovate with cuisines, there was no stopping me. I wanted to know what the chefs were cooking, not for their guests but for themselves in the executive kitchen – and it is from there that I would demand a piece of fish, a leg of lamb or a bowl of *dal* for lunch.

Welcomgroup had started a great tradition of presenting the regional cuisines of India, and I became party to this with much enthusiasm. What I enjoyed most was traditional Indian cooking, and I hope that the ITC hotel kitchens have benefitted from the research I initiated into its many secret variants, working with the finest food consultants and scholars. The hotels hired cooks who were not trained chefs from hotel schools – though there were those too – but were people who recognized the cuts and textures of flesh through touch alone.

When I look back at my career, its heights allow me a certain satisfaction, in the legacy of some of the finest hotels and restaurants that were created, and in establishing ITC as a serious player in the hotel industry with a distinctly Indian dimension.

If the hotel kitchens were experimental, the kitchen at home was a laboratory too. Spices were ground fresh, meats pounded, and discussion hovered often enough around how to cook a curry, or what to add to a *korma*. Sukhi swore that just listening to all the talk about food was enough for her to put on weight, which no one took seriously for she was both petite and delicate.

When Gori was small, she was reared on bread and milk and, later, on 'Dog Cerelac'. As she became a little older, she was weaned away from a puppy's diet with soupy broths that consisted of chopped vegetables, meat stock, and calcium and vitamin supplements, alternated with bowls of liver and mince. A lot of dog owners ask the butcher for those bits and blobs that are usually thrown away, to turn to stock, or add to their pets' food, but mindful of her health, I had instructed the servants that Gori was not to be fed on such scraps.

In my view, there is nothing that comes close to the excellence of Indian cuisine. It is for me both gourmet as well as comfort food. If I liked Mughlai food, Gori loved it too. She'd soon realized that I was a softie in matters of food. If I sat at a table groaning with food, I could hardly refuse to share it with those I loved. And there was no doubt that among those I counted as my loved ones, Gori came pretty high up in the hierarchy.

So, bad habit or not, Gori enjoyed the rich pickings of the table. Whenever I sat down for a meal, you could bet that Gori would be by my feet. If there were guests and I got carried away in a conversation, Gori would either look up or, not getting the kind of response she hoped for, would nudge my leg, as if to say, 'Okay, enough talking, what about something nice for me instead?'

And so Gori got hooked on to the taste of *galotis* and *kakori kebabs*, *biryanis* and *nalli kormas*. Even though I ensured that I only gave her small, digestible bits, Sukhi would complain that I was sure to ruin her health this way. So I took to wiping the tidbits in tissue paper to remove excess oil and spices before bending down to feed her, and sometimes I'd ask for warm water to wash joints and bones for her.

On days we were hosting parties, Gori would be in a state of ecstasy. Even though we usually ate well, parties at our home tended to be sumptuous feasts with an array of flesh and meat dishes in incredible concoctions of the kind that might have graced the tables of the Mughals and the Deccani nawabs. For Gori, the day would begin with delight, as aromas – one more delicious than the other – wafted throughout the house. On those days, she'd forsake even her afternoon siesta to nose around the kitchen, hoping to find something carelessly dropped, or a benevolent Agnes on a break relenting sufficiently to surreptitiously feed her a piece of chicken or lamb.

Sukhi would object to Gori's presence on my guest list, not because she was a nuisance – if anything, Gori revelled in company – but because she'd enjoy the freedom to stake out the guests. Those who talked to her, or petted her, she realized were a soft touch, so when dinner was served, she made sure to go sit by their side. I never saw her misbehave, but it's not easy on the conscience of most to nibble on a tender sliver of meat, or suck deep on a marrow bone, without feeling guilty about a pair of eyes watching your every move. Sooner or later, they'd relent and slip her a tasty morsel or an unchewed bone, and

Gori would be in heaven – but only momentarily, before she transferred her affections to the next diner. Others, I am sure, as Sukhi often pointed out, probably kept their silence at a dog's presence in their midst only because they were mindful of their manners and in deference to their hosts.

Aamir Raza Hussain was not among them.

Most people know Aamir on account of his contribution to theatre. Several of his more important directorial ventures were presented by Welcomgroup, and were probably the most lavish spectacles undertaken in India. These include the spellbinding *Legend of Ram* and *The Kargil War*, which had to be staged outdoors with a special auditorium that moved on tracks!

Interested as I was in his work, more useful for me was Aamir's access to the Rampur archives – he is a nephew of the Nawab of Rampur – as well as to cooks who would take the development of Dum Pukht cuisine to another level altogether.

Particularly on festive occasions, Aamir was given to dropping in with special delicacies from his house – *sevaiyan* and *kebabs*, *kormas* and *kaliyas* – that I looked forward to almost as much as Gori did. While Gori got her share of the goodies, what she was never able to resolve was the whole paradox of Aamir, who disliked dogs and would lift his feet away if Gori so much as came around to where he was sitting. Allowing her a lick of gratitude was too far-fetched to even think of, a pat was difficult to imagine considering he could hardly bear to be in the same room as her. So much so, it was only when Aamir was coming over that Gori would be chained. Much though she resented it, she also looked forward to the treats that Aamir carried with him.

Years later a colleague, a regular at my parties, pointed out that Gori seemed to know seconds ahead of my seeking her out in any such gathering, and she'd be looking at me from across the room, or garden, whenever I turned towards her. It was as though there was a mysterious connection between us.

If Gori enjoyed her hors d'oeuvres with the guests, she had her main course with me. One of my peculiar habits was my inability to dine with my guests. I would sit down to dinner not just after everyone had eaten, but mostly after everyone had been seen off to their cars. I liked my meal uninterrupted, and usually had it with only Gori for company. My staff knew that on these occasions a bowl of warm water was always to be kept beside my plate, in which I would wash the meats and bones before they found their intended receptacle in Gori's greed.

On all such occasions, as Sukhi supervised the winding up operations, she'd crib about Gori's unhealthy eating habits. 'She'll be sick,' which was an understatement, for she'd usually suffer a major tummy upset after these lavish meals. Inevitably, the following day, her diet would consist of yoghurt and *isabgol* (psyllium husk) along with a tablet of Zinetac.

After the party, the medicine – but at least it didn't leave a bitter aftertaste in Gori's mouth.

I had never thought of Gori as a thief. It was when she was much older that the servants disclosed the truth.

'At first,' said Agnes, 'I'd scold Vishnu for putting out the butter-dish without any butter in it.'

Apparently, Gori was partial to the taste of butter, and when no one was looking, wasn't above getting herself a lick.

'Ooh,' said Sukhi, when they recounted the tale, 'I wonder how many times we've had butter that she had tasted first.'

Gori was put up to these antics by Baba, about whom more later. Suffice it to say that she would jump from a stool on to a chair and the dining table. She was fond of fruit and though it was a staple part of her diet, whenever she felt peckish, she would swipe an apple or a mango from the fruit-bowl.

Much though she feared Diwali crackers, she loved the goodies that accompanied the explosive sounds. 'Once,' said Vishnu, 'I caught her polishing off a whole box of Diwali cookies.'

'And I thought it was the servants,' said Sukhi sheepishly.

A Romance Gone Sour

Though we never spoke openly about it, Sukhi and I were both keen that Gori have puppies and raise a family. Nor was Gori averse to romance herself. On our morning walks, though the street dogs tended to be loutish, there was one handsome rogue she seemed keen on. In the days before I started to keep her on a tight leash, she'd amble over and flirt outrageously with the street Romeo.

Through our vet we found a family that had two male Spitz studs and were as keen to have them crossed as we were. Since we had the female of the species, etiquette demanded that we should ferry Gori across to their residence, a task that a friend undertook on our behalf. Right from the start, though, Gori appeared uninterested in the dogs. Perhaps she needed to be courted in style, and the presence of not one but two males, who seemed content playing with each other while passing rude remarks in her presence, may have been upsetting.

In any case, nothing happened.

The owner of the males, a Mr Gupta, suggested that Gori be left alone with the dogs. The next morning, and then again a day later, Gori was driven across for what should have been a romantic interlude, but she refused to be drawn in by the males.

Maybe she wasn't attracted to them. I worried that all the pampering meant that she was no longer looking for love. Would she never get pregnant?

One of the games I'd play every day with Gori, and which had developed into a ritual, involved my unfolding a laundered shirt. As I'd get ready for my bath, she'd settle herself right next to the door – not just to keep guard but to enact a tug-of-war without which no working day was complete at least for Gori.

The laundry would fold my shirts crisply, using a thin cardboard collar to ensure that they did not crease. As I'd unfold a freshly laundered shirt after my bath, the temporary collar would fall down, which is what Gori would be waiting for. She'd grab the collar, I'd try to yank it away, she'd snatch it right back, and so it would go on for a couple of minutes, the game never varying, and lasting as long as it took for the collar to be torn apart, or until I let her win – which she enjoyed. On the few occasions when I snatched the collar away, she's be unhappy and bark till, in mock submission, I'd hand the trophy back to her, to her delighted wagging. Sometimes I'd twist the collar, so it was difficult to tear, playing out the game longer. And sometimes I'd unfold two, or even three, shirts just so that Gori could prolong our game.

While we played tussle, it was Vishnu's job to iron out the folds in the shirt. Expectedly, I'd be running late for a meeting, so I'd reprimand him for taking too long with the task. Though he never said anything to me, he complained to Sukhi that if I was all that particular about being punctual, why didn't I select the shirt the previous evening so he could iron and put it on a hanger without being accused of delaying Sahib who, he muttered into the palm of his hand, seemed to not mind wasting time playing with the stupid mutt? If Gori didn't like Vishnu, perhaps the feeling was mutual.

At any rate, spoiled silly by our little games and jousts, you could hardly blame Gori for finding it difficult to fall in love with a lesser being. Where was she to find someone who would love her as much and entertain her in the bargain?

Finally, it was among Sukhi's mahjong crowd that we found another Spitz owner, and once more Gori was hauled over to be mated – this time successfully.

Gori was five years old now. We celebrated the confirmation of her pregnancy, but Gori was unhappier than you would expect a mother-to-be to be. We put her moping down to hormones. The vet, the friendly but reticent Dr Pradeep Rana, who had attended to her since her arrival in our house, prescribed her a course of extra supplements and vitamins. But instead of glowing, Gori became increasingly withdrawn. Agnes increased her quantity of food and tidbits, but Gori ate only as much as she liked, often leaving tasty morsels untouched.

Dr Rana did an x-ray and gave us the happy news that Gori's litter would consist of three puppies.

'We could give away one,' I said to Sukhi.

'We'll keep one,' Sukhi was delighted but not ready to relinquish the reins of the house to a dopey husband.

When all seemed to be going well, at least for us, sometime, unknown to us, Gori aborted her puppies. We never ever found a trace of the foetuses though I ordered a search and myself looked high and low for them. One day the x-ray showed three puppies curled up in her womb, the next time she was taken to the vet for her examination, and another x-ray, they were gone. And Gori wouldn't stop bleeding.

Having lost her puppies, an infection in her uterus caused her to bleed profusely.

'She should be neutered,' Dr Rana advised us.

Back home, Sukhi and I discussed the implications of his directive.

'She got pregnant,' Sukhi started to say…

'…she can have puppies,' I completed on her behalf.

'We want her to try and become a mother again,' we told the vet, who looked unhappy.

After she'd aborted her litter, Gori continued to bleed heavily for several days. We'd clean up using pethidine, but nothing stopped the heavy flow. Her pain was accentuated by not being allowed on to the bed. I'd stop by Pradeep's clinic on my way to work in the mornings, Gori lying on sheets of newspaper in the backseat, no longer putting her face out of the window to enjoy the breeze. He would prescribe a dose of medicines, and the flow would stop, or at least slow down, for a few days, before resuming again.

'She needs to have her uterus removed,' Pradeep would sigh, and look down at his notes. He truly hated communicating unhappy news.

'Not right now, maybe after she's had her first litter,' I'd counter.

'She will have puppies,' I said to Sukhi.

'She will have puppies,' Sukhi agreed.

When, some months later, Gori was still bleeding and weak from it, Sukhi and I realized there was no recourse to the vet's alternative.

'She'll never have babies,' Sukhi sobbed gently.

'We'll never see her puppies,' I agreed sadly.

Rather than see her weaken rapidly, and put her through the loss of so much blood, both of us relented, and on his surgery morning, Dr Anil Sood gave her a shot of anesthesia at Pradeep's clinic, and soon after, her uterus was removed.

I don't think Sukhi and I were ever sorrier, or sadder.

Time passed, the years rolled by. Gori and I continued to play tussle, we went together on our morning walks, but she was no longer as carefree, nor were Sukhi and I getting any younger.

Once again, it was Sukhi who took the gauntlet in her hands.

She found another puppy to bring home.

It wasn't as though Gori was old – she was only seven years, for heaven's sake – but it was what friends described as the twilight years. In light of her illness, we were also more acutely aware of the eventuality of losing her at some point in the future.

Baba was of better lineage than Gori, a handsome fellow who, some years earlier, might have been a willing, even gallant, suitor for her, but with her disinterest in romance and her uterus removed, was simply a far younger sibling, for want of another word to describe their friendship.

Where Gori had been compliant, Baba was naughty.

It seemed just the right combination to cheer her up and bring her out of the gloom that seemed to have descended on her.

While Gori had been smuggled in, Baba came after a lot of thinking on our part. I had long ago gotten over my pig-headedness about larger breeds, and recognized that Gori needed a companion to play with, who should be someone of her own kind.

Sukhi's reasoning was more practical. It was 2002, Gori was now seven years old and entering the august years of her life, and another pet would ease the pain of her passing away, which was inevitable. Rather than look for a new pet after that sorrowful event, she decided it was better to have another pet at home who would mask the hurt of such an eventuality.

Our reasons were sound, but how would Gori, cosseted and spoilt, and the centre of attention of our household, accept a trespasser?

We would soon find out.

Friends warned us of the perils of bringing in a new pup without due warning. A jealous dog might maul a small pup, they cautioned. Gori might become insecure, withdrawn, pine for the care she was accustomed to. She might resent the intruder.

Like parents, we were guided to initiate a bonding ritual between the old inmate and the new incumbent.

First bring the new pup's blanket home and leave it around for Gori to smell.

Introduce the pup to Gori gradually.

Leave the pup in a basket for Gori to smell and see, but divert all attention to Gori herself and don't make a fuss over Baba.

Let Baba sleep in his basket in another bedroom

No, no, make sure Baba slept in the same room as Gori but at a distance, or in a dog cage.

Let Gori play with Baba.

Don't let Gori play with Baba.

By the end, we were exhausted by the possibilities of what might, or might not, happen.

Full of apprehension and foreboding, Baba was brought home. His basket was placed in the guest bedroom. Gori was brought in. Would the heavens fall down on us?

Gori sniffed the intruder, seemed to like his smell, wagged her tail and turned to look at us, as if to ask, 'So what's the fuss about?' Perhaps the pup reminded her of her own aborted litter?

Whatever the reason, just like that, Baba became a part of Gori's and our lives.

Maybe because he was male, or because he hadn't come through the unfortunate set of circumstances that had guided Gori's entry to our home, or merely because it was his nature, Baba was naughtier than Gori had been at that age. He chewed up the edges of carpets and gnawed at slippers, tore at socks, and when a little older, would wolf down Gori's food before she could get to it. He'd be cuffed behind his ears for his frequent misdemeanours, but remained uncommonly cheerful. He was a good dog with a good heart and soon became an inseparable part of the household.

Like Gori, he slept on the bed, only he would try and monopolize the whole bed for himself and edge Gori off. On our morning walks, he'd tug at his leash, bark at other people, and try to draw attention to his pranks. At home, he too became part of Gori's rituals of seeing me off when I left for work and greeting me on my return. But he would break the queue, clamouring to be the first to get a hug, demanding his affections.

In all this, Gori behaved like the mature and elegant lady that she now was. She seemed to understand that the younger dog's mischievousness was his way of seeking notice in a household that otherwise revolved around her. I was conscious, too, that I would need to be measured in my response to Baba's constant and Gori's quieter demands. I was busier than ever before at work, and now my attention at home was split between the two. But precedence was always given to Gori, which she acknowledged. She seemed to have got a measure of Baba soon enough, and instinctively understood that my attention to Baba was more out of consideration for the young, which she handled with the maturity and grace that I had now come to associate with her. Not by even a degree did her warmth towards me waver. But then, not by even a degree did she feel threatened by my inclusion of Baba into our charmed circle.

Years later, Shagun would tell me that Baba had tried to become Gori till he realized that however much I loved him, he could not usurp for himself the very special place she held in my heart. 'Gori was like your child,' she would marvel.

Gori was top dog and she knew it.

Even though she was seven years older than Baba, Gori acquired a growing sense of playfulness with his arrival. No longer were her days at home spent snoozing quietly. While she did not join him in his roguish ways, she joined him at play. In any case, there were all his newer toys that were so much more fun than her own, older ones.

Baba grew fast and was soon larger than Gori's delicate frame. One of his favourite toys was a hard ball I had got for him from a pet shop in Hong Kong, though I realized later that it was hardly the right size and should have been a little smaller. Because he was fond of it, Baba would swagger around the house with the ball held in his mouth, as he loafed through the rooms or ran out into the backyard to scare away the birds, dropping it only to bark at them.

Gori was just as intrigued by the new ball. While she was unable to snatch it away from Baba's jaws, the moment he'd drop it on the floor, she'd snatch it and run off with it, leading to a merry chase around the house.

Fortunately for her, I was at home when, in the excitement of their games, the ball got lodged in her mouth. It was too large for her to spit out, and with it stuck behind her teeth, she began choking slowly. At first I dismissed the strange sounds I heard emanating from some part of the house as the normal consequence of having two dogs at home. But when the sounds persisted and became increasingly panicky, I went out to explore and found Gori struggling to get the ball out of her mouth. Her desperate facial contortions and bulging eyes were indicative of a near-fatal mishap. In the nick of time and with a great deal of difficulty, I managed to pry out the ball from where it was wedged.

Having forced her mouth open and maneuvered it out, I immediately chucked the offending ball into the trash can, but it would be many days before Gori ventured to play with her or Baba's toys again.

She may have been scared off toys for a while, but if there was one thing Gori enjoyed, it was teaming up with Baba to extract revenge for a humiliation that had festered in her heart over the years.

She had never forgotten the tomcat that had smacked her right in her face when she was younger. Nor had the tomcat, having established his victory, cared to mend his ways.

Now, with Baba by her side, she would stalk the cats that came into the backyard, Baba providing cover while she led the charge. The tomcat, which had enjoyed the run of the backyard with his harem and buddies, was now chased off and the territory reclaimed.

The vanquished enemy gave up sauntering through our garden. Gori had extracted her revenge.

An Ode to Gori

What most might consider an unusual household was, for me, an emancipated one. Many saw it only through the prism of its generous hospitality, but for me the relationships that were nurtured among all its inmates were equally important. I married again, and with Sahiba in my life, found myself a step-father to her daughter, Kimi, and son, Princy. If life at home had its ups and downs, the children, every one of them, accepted Gori as part of the family, and she quickly became everyone's favourite pet.

Unfairly for Vishnu, he was regarded as a bit of a pariah since he had failed to worm his way into Gori's affections. Was there something she sensed that we didn't know of the unfortunate fellow?

Whatever the reason, Vishnu would caustically refer to Gori as 'Madam'. In 2001, when Sukhi and I were travelling to America, we'd asked Sukhi's daughter Candy – Shagun's mother and a hotelier – to check on Gori as often as she could.

I remember Candy telling us, on her return, how she'd come home to find Agnes in the kitchen.

'Madam is in the bedroom,' Vishnu had said to her. True to

his word, Candy found Gori in our room, resting her head on the pillow.

After checking with Agnes that she was eating well and not in need of anything, and having played with her a little, she set out to leave. Gori followed her to the verandah. 'She looked at me so soulfully, I couldn't just abandon her there,' Candy told us. 'So I put her in my car and we went out for a drive and some shopping before coming back home.' After that, Candy made it a habit to drop by every day, not easy for her, simply because Gori made it worthwhile and lavished her with so much love in return.

Looking in on Gori was a task, Candy told us, she didn't mind performing at all.

It was Candy's daughter, Shagun, who had first made the connection. She pointed out what should have been obvious to everyone else too. Gori could sense I was on my way home before anyone else, even the guard, knew my car was approaching the gate.

'There we are, watching all that nonsense that Nani likes on television,' Shagun pointed out one evening, 'and I'm trying to snatch the remote away from her' – it's true, Sukhi was addicted to the most melodramatic soap operas there were – 'when all of a sudden Gori will cock her ears up, look towards the door, and bolt towards the entrance.' Everyone thereafter confirmed that seconds before the driver tooted the horn for the guard to open the door, Gori would know I was home.

I'm not sure when I started noticing art, but I certainly became conscious of it with every new hotel that ITC built. In each case, contemporary artists were invited to be part of the projects, and it was a learning experience to see how local architectural practices were modified to create modern relevance. Art and landscaping were inseparable elements of the architecture.

We had also taken the lead in organizing art camps at several of our locations during the low-activity summer months. This allowed me the opportunity to see artists at work, follow their creative processes, and understand their language, which not everyone seemed to understand or relate to. From following their work to acquiring their work was one short step, aided by the fact that prices then were not as stratospheric as they are now. Pretty soon, the walls at home were covered by paintings that were often the subject of lively discussions when we had friends over, with many exclaiming that they couldn't understand head or tail of what they were about and my confessing that neither did I, really.

I wondered what they'd have thought if I had told them that I was contemplating getting a portrait done by a contemporary artist. Not of our ancestors, or of the family, as most people might have considered. My preference of subject for the only painting I have ever commissioned was slightly unconventional – Gori.

My selection of Subrata Kundu as the artist was based on several factors.

I had seen him work in the 1990s and was impressed by his dedication, as well as the way he used a set of images to create a collage-like painting.

I was not being merely paradoxical in choosing to have Gori instead of a loved human as the focus of the canvas. It is my belief that we Indians are umbilically linked to our homes. Maybe because we spend our lifetimes (and our lifetime's savings) to build our dream home, and are reluctant to sell and buy houses as casually as people in the West tend to do, we invest them with a great deal of emotion and feelings. Yet, when it comes to documenting these same homes, we tend to be neglectful.

My brief to Kundu, therefore, was to create a painting about all the things I considered dear to me. These consisted of the house but without its residents, not because I loved them any less, but because we had so many other ways of recording each other's presence, not least through hundreds or thousands of photographs that we seemed to take all the time.

'I want,' I said to an amused Kundu, 'a portrait of my house.'

Kundu had been completing some work at Lalit Suri's house in the vicinity. Lalit was a fellow hotelier, and therefore a competitor, but also a friend. To Kundu's credit, he did not laugh at my idea. At least not to my face.

It was decided that we would begin the process by taking photographs of the house. Kundu set to work, marching around the exterior spaces – taking pictures of the front, side and rear elevations, the entrance and garden, the greenery, and interior close-ups of the living room, even the bedroom and kitchen. Choosing what would be used and eliminating others was difficult, though in the end, restricted by a canvas that was ten feet by four feet, we decided to drop the kitchen and bedroom. Playing around the final selection, in jigsaw-like combinations, we placed Gori's picture at the centre of the assemblage. I was ready to give Kundu the go-ahead.

Reactions among the family ranged from the incredulous to the exclamatory. I suspect some may have thought I'd lost my marbles. 'How's the painting going?' I'd be constantly ribbed. I was determined to have the last laugh.

Three months later, Kundu was ready to unveil his masterpiece. Using oil on canvas, Kundu had invested the colours with a deep resonance and captured the essence as well as the warmth with which I viewed my living spaces. Arranged similarly to the collage of photographs we'd approved, Gori gloriously basked in the centre of the painting. As an artistic collaboration, it was perfect. I felt my chest bursting with pride.

Sukhi must have agreed with me, for the painting was given the pride of place in the living room, so prominently placed that no one could miss it in a room full of many other paintings.

I paid Kundu handsomely for the commission. But it was a small price to pay for my ode to Gori, who was thus immortalized on canvas in her adopted home.

The Worst Years of My Life

We are perhaps fortunate that we live our days unknowing of the sorrows that await each one of us ahead.

Two thousand three is a year I'd like to forget. India was 'shining', the economy was booming, financial investment was pouring in, the whole world wanted a slice of the action, and the hospitality sector had never had it better. ITC was on an expansion spree. We were renovating properties and rooms and adding hotels in places where we'd never had a presence. I was often in Mumbai, where two ITC projects – the Grand Maratha and the Grand Central – were occupying my time.

In the midst of this, Sukhi fell seriously ill. She was diagnosed with severe pneumonia. She had difficulty breathing and her movements were severely restricted. For most of July she was in hospital. When she came home, doctors advised that she be protected from all possible infections, and our bedroom was isolated and turned into her recuperation chamber.

Sukhi complained that she felt like a prisoner, but was too weak to see her threat of marching right out to take charge of the house, through. I tried to spend as much time as possible at home. Candy and Shagun came often. Even though we tried to be cheerful in front of Sukhi and even each other, from being an infectiously happy household, we'd soon descended into being an infectiously depressing lot. A portrait of the house, had Kundu painted it now, would have been a cheerless one.

How much of this did Gori comprehend? She'd been baffled by Sukhi's absence while she was away at hospital. She was more used to my comings and goings, but why was her mistress away? She could probably smell her on our clothes as we came and went from the hospital, and must have found the medicinal odours upsetting.

But all this was nothing compared to the forlornness she must have experienced when Sukhi returned. Suddenly, she was no longer allowed into her bedroom where Sukhi was quarantined, or anywhere around Sukhi, and as I increasingly spent more time with the patient, she must have found my abstinence from her company discomforting. Yet, Gori's behaviour towards us never changed. I saw her sense of curiosity about the peculiar goings-on give way to understanding, then reconciliation and acceptance. Something was abnormal, and along with Baba, she would have to learn to cope with it, just as all of us too were managing the best way we could.

When she was rushed once again to the hospital, none of us knew that we would not be seeing Sukhi alive at home again.

When her body was brought back for her loved ones to see one last time, Gori and Baba were locked away in our bedroom.

Unlike us, they were lucky not to see Sukhi in a state of eternal rest.

Gori was already nine years old, and though the years had so far been easy on her, sorrow now settled heavily about her. For a while after Sukhi's death, she appeared lost, and never recovered her joie de vivre again. She'd still leap up with joy when she saw me, she still loved a good feed under the table, but the happiness seemed to have seeped out of her. She was now quieter and in the unexplained absence of her day-time parent, drew increasing succour from Baba and the household staff. Agnes reported that she no longer enjoyed going out for long walks, and would often crawl under my bed, or the sofa, to hide. She was also sluggish on our morning walks, and at night nestled ever closer to me every time I turned over in my sleep.

By now, the foods division of ITC had been placed under my charge, requiring me to travel even more than before. With new hotels underway in Kolkata and Mumbai, I was spending less and less time in Delhi, and Gori, left alone over longer periods, was spending more time in Baba's company.

Mumbai was a strategic market and required my presence, which I gave willingly. By the time 2005 rolled around, the re-merger of ITC Hotels with its parent company had been accomplished. The opening of the Grand Maratha, with its historically-blended architecture so reminiscent of the Bombay of a century ago, had been a huge success. The Grand Central too had opened and had proved a greater challenge since it was located in what was then considered down-market Lower Parel, though the area has since boomed. People laughed at the project at the time, but it kicked off the renaissance of that part of the city, which is now a thriving commercial address.

Delhi, meanwhile, was getting warmer. Every April, residents of the capital are caught by surprise at how soon the short spring turns into a long summer. Every year they complain that the heat seems to have set in earlier, and every year the heat seems sharper, fiercer. Truth is, April catches us unawares, and it is May by the time we reconcile to the heat, wilting in its onslaught. In April 2005, I was too often away, and my mind occupied, to worry about how hot it had got. I do recall that Gori and Baba were often in my bedroom with the air-conditioning on, though they would dutifully trot out to see me off, and to greet me. Agnes would faithfully report on the housekeeping and the dogs' health.

I wonder now, if I had been more vigilant, I might have detected the poison that would destroy Gori's life.

It is now clear that it was sometime in late April or early May that Gori picked up an infection, though she exhibited no outward symptoms of it at the time. If there was a temporary loss of appetite, it would have been explained away by the heat. But Agnes, who fed both the dogs, did not spot anything unusual in her behaviour.

Not till the middle of May, that is, when she reported to me that both Gori and Baba had been occasionally passing dark stools. I instructed her to ask the driver, John, to take her and the dogs to Dr Pradeep Rana for a check-up.

Agnes had already, wisely, adjusted their diet not just for the summer but also for what she considered a digestive problem, substituting flesh and stock with curds and *isabgol*, and increasing vegetables in their broth. The vet agreed that the heat was the probable cause, and asked Agnes to continue giving them a lighter diet, and prescribed medication for their upset stomachs.

Agnes explained as much to me in Mumbai. Now that Gori had Baba for company, I had given up my habit of speaking to her over the phone from outside town, and was satisfied that they seemed to be recovering. At least, Baba recovered completely, but Gori, after showing initial signs of improvement, resumed passing dark stools, and when I returned home from Mumbai, I saw that she had begun vomiting too.

It was 28 June when I took Gori to Dr Rana, hoping to get to the bottom of her raging infection. Gori had become less frolicsome with age, and the purging had weakened her, but I could see nothing that worried me, nor did Dr Rana say anything that set the alarm bells ringing. He did want a blood-stool-urine test done, though, the results for which would need to be obtained from a pathology lab.

How much we humans take for granted. For us, these mandatory checks are second nature, and we easily provide samples for them, never considering how difficult it might be for other creatures to do so.

Just how difficult it could be, I was to discover for myself very soon.

Blood? Check. No problem there. It would be drawn at the pathology lab using a syringe, the same as for us humans.

Stool? Check. As soon as Gori had done her job, a sample could be collected in a plastic pouch.

But urine? How were we to collect an uncontaminated sample? In the twenty-four hours before I found myself back at Dr Rana's, I'd realized it was going to be impossible to get Gori to urinate in a test-tube.

Rana injected Gori with a diuretic at eight o'clock that night, advised me to force her to drink a lot of water, and asked the compounder to give me a syringe with which to collect her urine from a sanitized area where she might need to be tied up.

It was easier said than done. I had Vishnu remove all the carpets from the bedroom. The floor was wiped first with a damp cloth, then with Listerine. Forcing her to lap up water from her bowl, I tied her to the foot of the bed on a short leash so she would not clamber up. And then, I sat down to wait. It was the first of many long and despairing nights.

I watched television, and then read a little – anything I could lay my hands on, magazines, books, even office papers. But it was many years since I had given up my night patrol duties in the army, so keeping awake was a more difficult task than I had originally thought. It was around four in the morning that Gori started squirming and agitatedly winding around in a cyclic pattern. She had never once soiled the house, and could not understand why I was not taking her out when she was so clearly in need of a toilet break. If it were not for the diuretic, she would not have sullied the floor, but unable to control the pressure on her bladder, she finally gave up and urinated.

I was up in a trice, using the syringe somewhat inexpertly to gather as many of the small rivulets of urine that flowed in different directions, syringing each one into a previously sanitised jar till I reasoned I had enough, while Gori looked on shamefacedly. Having put it aside and sponged down Gori as best as I could, I was able to retire for a few hours of sleep before bed-tea and the morning routine of the house roused me. Having bathed and dressed, I had the urine sample delivered to the path lab, and went off to work.

The following evening, armed with all the reports, I was back at Dr Rana's.

Pradeep Rana is one of the most soft-spoken persons I have known and is one of Delhi's most popular vets with a flourishing practice in Niti Bagh. At any time, on any day, his clinic is filled with dog owners and their wards of all shapes and sizes, colours and hues, gathered for routine examinations or serious surgeries. To all of them, he holds out hope like a slender string.

Over the years, his had become a familiar face as first Gori, then Baba, visited his clinic for their routine shots and minor ailments. But now, as he looked at Gori's reports, his face turned passive. Once more he quizzed me on her symptoms, shook his head, then as gently as he possibly could, he delivered the verdict that both her kidneys had been badly affected.

Gori's was a case of close to acute renal failure.

I must have looked unbelieving.

'Let me explain,' he said, and true to his word, he set out Gori's prognosis. 'The good lord,' he said, 'in his wisdom, when he created dogs, gave them two kidneys just like he did to human beings.' Because one kidney takes over from the other in case of infection or when one stops functioning, they do not immediately show symptoms of infection or disease. Besides, the body is able to take a good deal of abuse, which is why there were no outward manifestations of anything wrong.

'But how did she pick up the infection?' I asked.

Pradeep Rana explained, 'It can reach inside anywhere from the vagina upward, go into the bladder and from there reach the kidneys, or enter from any other route through the bloodstream.'

Clearly, there was no way to protect pets from it, and Dr Rana confirmed as much. 'It is one of the biggest problems of a canine practice,' he shared his knowledge patiently, though I could see that a long queue of patients was waiting for their turn with the vet. 'Pets might exhibit some symptoms, but we're usually unable to catch them. Unlike humans, who can explain their discomfort, with a dog an infection might only become obvious once they start having intestinal disturbances such as vomiting or diarrhea.'

I was shaken. So, maybe – I still thought *maybe* – Gori was showing signs of renal failure, but that did not mean both her kidneys were totally gone. Surely, with medicines and nursing, she would recover?

'I'll prescribe a course of antibiotics,' Pradeep Rana got busy scribbling on his letterhead, 'she'll need to be brought here for her saline drips.'

I nodded. Gori was temporarily unwell. I resolved to nurse her back to health.

Meanwhile, I wanted to make sure that the path lab hadn't botched up the results, so with another diuretic injected into her, I sat on a vigil once more. Once more I syringed the urine spilling in different directions, and took the sample to another path lab, but with minor differences – possibly accounting for the medicines she had begun taking – the result was the same.

Just as Dr Rana had warned me, Gori became increasingly sluggish and lethargic, and soon lost her appetite. No sooner had she eaten, she would vomit. 'You need to put more food into her,' Dr Rana said at his clinic, where she was now being taken every morning and evening for saline drips.

If feeding her was a problem, keeping her from water in what was turning into a hot and parched summer was even more difficult. 'She needs to be kept away from drinking water as much as possible,' Dr Rana explained, because it made her nauseous and no sooner had she lapped up some, she would start heaving and retching.

Between John, Vishnu, Agnes and I, we devised some creative menus for her, food that was at least nourishing even in small quantities, and which she would hopefully retain. Because conventional food now repulsed her, we would give her a little ice-cream (which used to be an occasional treat earlier), or mango pulp, which she had always loved, or mashed banana, while I watched her face for some signs of satisfaction with her new nutritional programme.

Keeping her from water was torturous. To let her have a minimum amount without causing her damage, I would put an ice-cube in a bowl and place it before her. She would lick the ice-cube greedily, thirstily – it was the littlest amount of water I dared give her, but at least she could enjoy it as long as the ice-cube lasted. It was difficult watching her, like a child in distress, and if I could, I would have readily taken on her condition to spare her the pain.

'She's suffering a lot, doctor,' I said to Pradeep Rana, who nodded – he didn't need to be told. What I did not share even with him was that I was now keeping a watch over Gori through the night. I was collecting urine samples every week, sitting up at night for the task, monitoring every little improvement, such as when her creatinine serum count, which indicated her renal function, fell, or despairing when it rose. As a result I'd got used to staying awake, unmindful of the toll it was taking on me. I just hoped to provide Gori with whatever little comfort I could offer her when she awoke in pain, wetting her lips or occasionally dribbling a few droplets of water on her tongue, as I held her and talked to her late into the night.

Then, in what had become a daily ritual, I would take her to the vet's clinic for her morning saline drip and medicines, exchanging a few words with Dr Rana on her condition or sharing the latest pathology reports while she was being hooked up, and then I'd leave for office. John would bring her back home, where she'd rest, and then take her back to the clinic in the evening, where I'd join them while returning from work.

'Will I be all right?' she seemed to say, looking at me for

assurance. 'You'll be just fine,' I would reassure her. 'I'm here, aren't I?'

Gori bore her lot stoically. I do not remember her whimpering when she was injected, pummeled, kept away from water and fed mini-meals that barely assuaged her hunger and thirst. As I sat talking to her in the bedroom, she would look up pathetically, as if to ask, 'What's wrong with me? Will I be all right? I will get okay, won't I?'

I prayed that she would, indeed, get okay.

But the answer was writ all over Gori's face. Initially, she made it known that she was aware – and grateful – for the care and attention she was receiving. Later, it was replaced by lethargy and indifference. For a while, I thought I spotted a sense of despair. Finally, it gave way to helplessness and resignation.

Gori was willing to let go, but not I.

If I could, would I have exchanged places with her, I couldn't help wondering.

'Once a dog's creatinine serum is over five, the prognosis is bad,' Dr Rana had warned me. Gori's creatinine serum, even as it varied, was around 12.10. Its reference range: between 0.20 and 1.50. 'She'll get better,' I promised him, even though I could tell the symptoms were not good.

'The damage to her kidney tissue is established,' he said, 'her prognosis is poor.'

'Check her medicines again,' I cajoled him. 'Something else is bound to make her better.'

On 30 June, he said he wasn't comfortable with her deteriorating condition, leaving everything else unsaid. That night, I held Gori in my arms for a long time, as I crooned to her.

My family, those who visited at home, and colleagues at work, commented that I was losing weight. I was, I knew, feeling the need to pull my belt a notch tighter. But I was no longer my own priority and my health would have to wait while I found a way to heal Gori. She could no longer walk even a few feeble steps, and would need to be carried whether to the vet's or occasionally outside, though not so much for obeying the call of nature as to get some fresh air.

By the middle of July, Dr Rana was no longer content with laying out hints – both Gori's distress and my own were obvious to everyone. 'She should be put to sleep,' he said gently.

'Her blood urea nitrogen count has improved,' I reminded him, 'maybe the next report will be even better.'

Dr Rana knew better than to argue with a pet owner. 'Breaking such news is always tricky,' he would tell me later, 'even when their pets have been unwell for a while, any talk of putting them down comes like a bolt from the blue.'

He'd given his verdict but hadn't given up on Gori. Her treatment continued.

By the third week of July, he was actively persuading me to have Gori put to sleep. By now, the struggle to stay alive had completely worn Gori down, but I was simply not prepared to let go. Gori had to live. Gori *must* live. I knew I was being unreasonable, but I could not prevent a streak of obstinacy from masking the inevitable.

'I will see you,' I said to Dr Rana with as much dignity as I could muster, 'in the morning tomorrow.'

On 27 July, I did not accompany John and Agnes to the vet as I had an important meeting in the morning at the office. Dr Rana,

who saw her, appeared resolute that Gori should be put to sleep there and then.

John, the good soul that he is, panicked. He had been party to innumerable such conversations between the vet and me, and remained unmoved by the doctor's logic, only to protest, 'Sahib, I cannot do it, or take the decision.'

Extraordinarily for him, Dr Rana was unyielding. 'There's no need for a drip or injections anymore,' he signaled to his team. 'We're only prolonging her pain.'

In the face of such stubbornness, John did the only thing he could. He switched on his mobile and connected me to Gori's vet.

A cold weight settled in the pit of my stomach.

Never before had I heard Dr Rana sound so stern.

'We've done all we could for her, Major Sa'ab,' he said. 'I know you're prepared to run with her till the very end but the time has come when we need to let her go for her own sake.'

Later, John told me that Gori's ears had pricked at the sound of my voice on the phone. Had her acute hearing made out that it was I on the phone, even though we were not on the speakerphone? After all, she was accustomed to my telephonic voice.

'Doctor,' I said, 'I'll come back early from office, and bring her to you as soon as I get back. I'd...' I know my voice faltered a little, 'I'd like her to pass away in my arms.'

Not willing to let go, I told him about a little spot in the wilderness close to the house that I had identified as Gori's final resting place.

Barely had they got home around noon that John called again. Gori was extremely restless, he said, and seemed to be searching for me everywhere. 'I think there is very little time left, Sahib,' he said. 'I think you should come home immediately.'

Had she perhaps sensed the finality of our conversation, I wondered, as I put down the receiver. Had she given up all hope?

'Oh, Allah,' I recalled a well-remembered quotation, 'give me the courage to change the things that I can, the serenity to accept those which I cannot, and the wisdom to know the difference.' I had my answer and knew what I had to do next.

My office was in Golf Links, less than half-an-hour's commute away, but when I reached my car, I found that my other driver, Chotu, had gone for lunch.

Not wanting to waste a moment more than was necessary, I sent for the keys, got into the driver's seat, and was soon on my way. 'Be sure to drive carefully,' I chided myself. 'Don't over-speed, don't be reckless,' perhaps trying to divert my mind with the mundaneness of driving away from what I knew awaited me at the journey's end.

Maybe if I had been faster, I might have seen Gori alive.

By the time I arrived home, Gori had died a few precious seconds earlier.

John was insistent that she had sensed my presence. She certainly seemed to have had more than a dog's sixth sense when it came to recognizing the sound of my car. Just as I had turned the corner that afternoon, the point from where her ears usually picked up the car's sound, John said she had barked violently, then jerked, and was no more.

Had she wanted to spare me the agony of dying in my arms? Or had she waited for me till her last breath and felt betrayed by my absence?

In the fleeting moments immediately after her passing away, and seeing her lifeless before me, I could sense the jigsaw puzzles of her life fitting together before my eyes – her playfulness as a puppy, her growing affection for me, her attachments and her wisdom. Her entire lifespan had played out before me as a conscious adult, and now I saw vignettes of it flash by in my mind as she lay lifeless in my arms. What I would have done then to breathe life into her, to shake her back into consciousness and existence.

Shutting her eyes with my hands, I ordered my suddenly silent staff to gather all her favourite toys and her feeding bowls. I wrapped her in her blanket, removed her collar – which I have preserved at home still – and prepared her for her final journey.

I would lay her to rest in a tree-shaded wilderness, close to the house that, for ten years, had been her home.

A House with a View

It was a coincidence that when I lost Gori, I was weighing various options of where to settle down, now that my retirement years were upon me. I can say with some satisfaction that I had packed my professional years with a certain amount of grace, and it was the same elegance I wanted to bring to bear on my twilight years.

Should I shift to Hyderabad? It was certainly a city with historical attractions, and had a pace that was charming. As the city of my birth and ancestry, I had, a decade previously, bought a half-acre of land on which to build a cottage, but now that the day of reckoning was close at hand, I wondered what to make of my decision to settle there. My brothers and sisters no longer had lasting links with that city. Many of them had settled abroad, most of them cocooned in the comfort of their children's and grandchildren's lives. Their visits, if any, to Hyderabad were now undertaken as visitors and no longer as residents. The family house at Himayat Nagar had been sold long ago, and subsequent houses bought by them had either been sold or leased. One brother had retained a house in Banjara Hills, the other had a house in the old city, and my sister had sold hers to a developer to turn into apartments. Older relatives had passed away, and I had few friends there.

Most of my own colleagues seemed to be making a beeline for Gurgaon, the Haryana suburb in the National Capital Region, which as the promised 'millennium city' seemed to strike a stronger chord with them as well as with me. Driven by that dream and wanting to be close to a small circle of professional friends and colleagues, in 2004 I bought two adjacent plots of a thousand square yards each in Gurgaon's Sun City. The acreage would be sufficient should I want to resurrect my dream of having kennels and a pack of dogs, the thought came unbidden to me.

I had gone to the extent of having plans for the house and kennels drawn up, when the first disquieting reports of a rapidly collapsing infrastructure began to dispel the euphoria of living in Gurgaon. Already some colleagues, serving and retired, had shifted there, but were increasingly unhappy with the civic services and utilities. Power outages lasted for hours. Water supply was inconsistent, and the ground water was disappearing as fast as the surrounding greenery. There was absolutely no public transport. Roads barely existed, were potholed or jammed with cars, and simply vanished every time it rained. What was scarier was that permissions for oncoming development of an astonishing magnitude had been given, and now loomed large. Gurgaon, already a mess, was not turning out to be the place I wanted to live in during my post-retirement years.

Fortunately for me, I had another ace up my sleeve.

I might have extended Gori's excruciating pain, but even when she was well I was aware that she was ageing, and every time I set out for a walk in the morning, I was reminded that in time I might lose her. This thought had become all the more persistent after Sukhi's demise. Mentally, I had decided that a scrub clearing where the last house of the colony petered out might be the place I would choose to bury her.

As luck would have it, the last house overlooking the wilderness that surrounded the fourteenth-century fort of Khilji that had been unoccupied for many years, came up for sale, but for a combination of reasons it was not enjoying much success in finding a buyer.

They had, of course, not reckoned with me.

For a start, the plot was not *vastu*-compliant, being wide in front and narrow behind. Its former occupants, I was informed – by brokers, naturally – had left with unsavoury accounts. Surely, it was suggested, I wanted something less formidable. What they didn't know was that for me, *vastu* is a set of scientific principles you bring into building a house that delivers light and air, and the principles had been formulated in an era when hygiene and sanitation systems were under-developed, and outbreaks of possible epidemics loomed large. Turning *vastu* into a set of complicated rituals had created a recipe for exploitation by the unscrupulous.

The plot's location next to the wilderness was also thought to be a disadvantage since it could be a security hazard. It must be said that the park at that time was being used by anti-social elements for illicit activities, but surely these were matters that could be attended to. In any case, having a plot of land open to greenery and a piece of history was to me romantic, much more of an advantage than a nuisance. Not that I would hint at anything of the sort to the seller!

There was also the matter of a school close to the plot, which resulted in a fair bit of traffic on that part of the road, especially in the mornings. I was not deterred by that either. I reasoned that 104 Saturdays and Sundays, almost two months of summer holidays, and other national and gazetted holidays, would account for at least 165 days. I would have only 200 days to contend with, and that too only the first half of the day. Surely that could hardly compare with the advantages of building a home for myself in that spot. Indecisive as I was about Gurgaon, I bought the Panchsheel Park plot, house and all, unsure of where it might lead me.

As chance would have it, it was facing this plot that, on the evening of 27 July 2005, John, Vishnu and I took turns digging a hole where, surrounded by her toys, and packed in salt so that wild animals would not get to her, we laid Gori solemnly to rest. I planted a tree a little to the side of the monument, both to mark the spot and as a memorial to her. A tree, I could not help thinking, was a symbol of life, and in planting this one in Gori's memory, I was playing my part in invigorating the city's ecological balance.

In that moment, when the earth had covered her and a small sapling raised its jaunty boughs to the rains, I knew precisely what I would do next.

I had a house to build that would overlook Gori's resting spot. It would be a cenotaph for her, my ode to the sentiment that bound us together. Living close to where she lay buried, I would be able to recount her memories whenever I chose.

It would be the house in which I hoped to spend the rest of my years, with Gori's final resting place in sight.

I was soon back to my routine, beginning my day with a walk that now included paying homage to Gori. Baba, who accompanied me, would sniff the sapling and wag his tail, almost as if he could sense Gori's presence there. On my part, I'd wish her a good morning, let her know I missed her, and that she should rest peacefully, and be off, various thoughts churning fiercely in my head.

The old house, I was sure, would need to be brought down.

Perhaps because of my ancestry, or simply because in my years at ITC Hotels I had been more sensitized than most regarding architectural heritage, I was sure that the house I would build would suggest a continuity with its fourteenth century Khilji lineage. After all, it would stand in the shadow of Allauddin Khilji's Siri Fort, at a spot where every speck of dust is steeped in history. Buried in the vicinity are remains of Mongol soldiers who ran amok all over Asia, from Siberia to China. But for Sultan Balban of the Slave Dynasty before him, and then Khilji, no Asian ruler had been able to stay their marauding armies, leave alone face their terrifying hordes. Nor was Khilji confined to just his capital in Delhi; after the Mauryans and before the Mughals, he was possibly the only ruler to have commandeered sovereignty as far as Bengal in the east and the Deccan in the south.

Building this house would not be easy. Strict regulations prescribed by the Archaeological Survey of India and the Municipal Corporation of Delhi had to be complied with. To their credit, these issues were professionally, expeditiously and helpfully dealt with, putting to rest the generally adverse public perception of these organizations.

It always irked me that Delhi, a city with more historical references than almost any other city in the world, was now bereft of any grand architectural design. Builders, owners, investors, architects, designers, each in their own way, had contributed to create an urban kitsch that in no way hinted at the five-thousand-year-old civilization we would so readily boast about. Even Banaras, with its dirt and filth and squalor, seemed to provide some sense of historical and architectural continuity that Delhi had gone to such lengths to eradicate.

Europe, on the other hand, had done so much to preserve its historical precincts. Italy, in particular, was my role-model, where even new structures had a resonance with the immediate environment, and old apartments or houses could be refitted inside but were not allowed to change their facades.

In my endeavour to build something linked with the city's cultural and architectural past, I was spurred on by the minister of tourism and culture, who at the time lived in the same neighbourhood.

'I'll build you a fitting memorial,' I promised Gori. 'It will keep your story alive.'

What I left unsaid was what I knew: that people would come to see the house also because they had heard its owner had built it specially to overlook the place where his dog lay buried.

Perhaps they might say that he was mad.

Perhaps they would say he was unique.

From the very beginning, I had a good deal of clarity about the kind of house I wanted to build at N-140, Panchsheel Park. Having always admired the building facades in Europe, and within the modest means at my disposal, I wanted to build a house that would be inspired by the city's syncretistic cultural heritage and might help trigger the kind of building skyline that would have a strong connect with the past. I wanted it to incorporate elements from the city's past architecture, borrowing from public structures, whether mosques or temples, but with a modern sensibility. It required a new architectural language. No architect's work, as far as I could glean from my research, offered what I wanted.

'It'll take time,' I whispered to Gori as I walked past her grave, 'but I will have my way.'

It became apparent to me that I would have to choose an architect to do my bidding rather than tell me what to do. I intensified my search and was lucky enough to find Ajay Govil and Paulomi D. Hazra of D.S.A. Consultants who had a history of building residences, though most would qualify as modern, even minimalistic in style, yet that did not deter me from briefing them on my requirements.

Ajay turned out to be a good sounding board. I told him I needed a façade in stone, culturally connected with Khilji's fourteenth century capital, which was also built of stone. Ajay quietly suggested some alternatives: Banswara pink stone, for instance, or the local Delhi quartz, picking black granite for the dark floors I wanted in the long dining room inspired by the castles of England. We looked at arches and domes, studied patterns of light, the slant at which it crept in winter, and the way it fell like a straight wash in summer.

We looked at the immediate topography, and knew instinctively that while the house would open on to the colony road, its views would offer unparalleled vistas of Siri Fort's walls – now fortuitously being cleaned up, and the wilderness 'beautified' with a garden and guards for security. I provided Ajay with magazine references and books. He drew sketches and showed me floor plans and C.A.D./C.A.M. drawings so I could walk 'virtually' through the spaces.

We decided on three levels for the house, the first of which would include a formal drawing room, a large bar-cum-den, and a separate and roomy dining room. The first floor would consist of four spacious bedrooms and a lounge, while the second floor would have my office, a guest bedroom next to it, a spacious en-suite master-bedroom consisting of a spacious bathroom, a walk-in wardrobe-cum-dressing room, and a personal study. All three levels would be held together by a courtyard atrium, the skylight diffusing the harsh Delhi light and spreading it through lobbies at different levels, to make the house as green and independent of electric lights as possible.

In fact, the architects had first submitted plans for the atrium consisting of three arches at the three different levels, but if I was not convinced, it was because it seemed a little too much to me. Eventually, I was able to guide them towards one long arch that emerged out of the gateway of the Purana Qila. Copper pipes were laid at the highest points of the atrium to create cooling curtains of mist that could be driven downwards to keep the house cool.

Nor did I want a sparse, spare house. India's great tradition of working with wood and stone is too rich to simply ignore in favour of the minimalistic style that has become fashionable nowadays, but which finds so little resonance in the country's history and culture. I wanted screens and stone trellises and carved features. The façade had to combine stone in a manner that was not simply derivative.

Poor Ajay and Paulomi. They would submit drawings and I would find fault with them. I was less than satisfied and made frequent changes in their submissions. I kept a notebook by my bedside for when inspiration, or just ideas, might strike. Slowly, but surely, different aspects of the house began to meld together. I might still quibble about the size of a window, or the need for a door, but it seemed that we had found a workable design. Certainly, Ajay and Paulomi were very efficient when it came to the details.

We were ready to roll.

I now understand why everyone is so excited, and exhausted, when they build their own house. The logistics are more than formidable. Not enough stone of a certain kind is available, or the contractor fails to supply it in the required size or width, the cement is of a different grade from that which was ordered, the cable wires will not take the sanctioned load and need to be changed, and the wood is not sufficiently seasoned as was promised. The labour takes off just when work is at its peak because it's festival time, or they are required at home to sow or reap, or because someone is getting married, or has died. Trucks are allowed into the city only at certain hours, and at night, when they're unloading, neighbours who were well within their rights to protest the noise, or because someone had got drunk and was carousing, bore it wonderfully and with fortitude.

Then there are all the decisions to be made, samples to be approved. How thick will the glazing be? Will the kitchen sink be steel or ceramic? There are the plumbing fixtures, the showers and faucets, to select, the light switches and fittings to spend hundreds of hours choosing, the electric fans, even the air-conditioning, to approve, the towel racks and door handles and, oh, so many, many things to go through, that at times it seems impossible the task will ever be completed. For those of you who have shared this journey, there is nothing new about these silly reminiscences. Even I, who had supervised the building of so many hotels for ITC, was finding myself getting bogged down building my own, much smaller house, on a far sparser budget. And this was before the furniture and furnishings could be chosen.

Then there was the landscaping to attend to, not that there was much of a garden space to talk about. Fortunately, the velvety green of the park, newly laid around the Khilji ruins, rolled right outside the house, but partly to soften the façade and keep it cool, and partly to make it look attractive, a garden was necessary. Realizing that the sun would not let any grass grow in the front yard, I decided on a raised garden, consisting of a green house completely webbed with mist pipes that would water plants growing down from suspended pots, while a series of gradients would create levels for a 'hanging' garden at the entrance to the house, which the drawing room would overlook.

Even as I write this, I am aware of the 'sprucing up' of the monument and the re-laying of the park, part of the beautification drive aimed at the Commonwealth Games in October 2010. It seems even the planets are conspiring to provide a face-lift to Gori's resting place. As a member of the Heritage Society of India, I have done my bit by further developing the park's aesthetics and lighting. The house too has been built using solid Burma teak, and one-and-a-half times the quantity of steel and cement required in the hope that it will last well into the future.

My morning walk now acquired a second detour as I checked each day's progress – it seemed so little. Slowly, from the foundations, the plinth began to rise, the walls were erected, the slabs of the ceilings were laid. I had my apprehensions as the stone cladding began – would it look gauche instead of classy? Every day, I reported the progress to Gori. Every week, I'd tell my bemused family, or friends, or colleagues, that I would soon move into the new house. In anticipation, I had the movers come and pack everything, as if by so doing I could hasten the process. That, sadly, did not happen, and I lived, for months, surrounded by cartons.

Slowly, my life at N-115, where I had stayed the longest in my life, was drawing to a close.

Just as surely as my life at N-140 was about to begin.

Requiem

I had disposed of my plots in Gurgaon's Sun City, convinced that I would not live there. After having begun work on the new house in Panchsheel Park, I realized I still needed a farmhouse, perhaps not for myself but for dogs who need open spaces to run and play. To that end, I bought another piece of farm land beyond Chhattarpur. I intend to begin building there some time soon, first a set of quarters for my staff who have given me many years of loyal service. Then the kennels – oh, but I forget, you don't know yet.

In April 2005, the month Gori had first exhibited early symptoms of her fatal illness, I had brought home a Spitz puppy with Sahiba's help to keep Baba company. Following Gori's death and the trauma associated with her illness and departure, I no longer wanted to be emotionally dependent on another pet to the same extent that I had become tied up with Gori. Baba and Robin, therefore, were dispatched to the kennel I had built for them in the driveway. Baba still had the run of the house, but this would diminish over time.

In May 2006, I did what I had wanted to do perhaps for years, a desire that had lain dormant all the time Gori was with me: I got home Dada, a handsome German Shepherd.

In July 2007, a female German Shepherd companion for Dada, Dasi, came home.

In the following months, having tracked a pair of Rampur Hounds to a family in Allahabad, Genghis and Jahan came home to the now-extensive kennels. I would tease my friend, Aamir Raza Hussain, who continued to come home with his festive treats, that the Rampur Hounds were a breed that had been concocted by his forefathers. Aamir, at least, remained immune to their charms.

In January 2008, I added two more Spitz from different litters, Bibi and Pilaru, to the menagerie.

In April 2008 I brought home Johnny, and in May 2008 Walker followed, both Labradors golden and black respectively, the colours associated with my own favourite sundowner, Johnny Walker whisky, mixed with single malts Talisker or Macallan.

In October 2008, Baba and Pilaru had a litter, from which I kept back one pup, christened Babu.

In June 2009, the Rampur Hounds had a litter, and I retained Jabeen.

In August 2009, Dada and Dasi had a litter of four pups, from which I gave away two, and Gabbar and Laila joined the kennel.

Agnes is now fully in charge of overseeing the welfare and wellbeing of the kennel. She is assisted by two full-time staff members, Ramanuj and Lincoln, and together they run a separate kitchen for the dogs. I am frequently asked by visitors about the quantity of rations required to feed this menagerie, but my staff says I should not disclose the amount. '*Nazar lag jayegi*,' they say. 'It will attract the evil eye.' So I pass over the matter, only sharing that it calls for hundreds of chapattis, several kilos of rice, vegetables and flesh, and in the summer, several litres of *dahi*.

A trainer comes in daily and spends two-and-a-half hours with the pack, and is generally happy with the result. Except, he claims, when I come around. Then there is chaos, the dogs misbehave, they tumble over each other to get to me, they fight with each other, or end up nipping at rumps and tails in friendly mock-fights. I make sure they are not loose when there are guests around, who, I am sure, would not enjoy the experience as much as I do.

They are a sight when they have to be walked. Nobody knows why I have fourteen dogs, or when I might add more to their numbers. Sometimes three or four people take them for walks together. At other times, Lincoln and Ramanuj walk them in turns. Either way, they are a sight to behold.

It has become difficult for me to take any one dog for a walk – the clamour and fighting that ensue make it impossible – so now I walk alone. I remember and mourn Gori all the more as a result.

Perhaps my neighbours wonder at my eccentric ways. Maybe they think I am a little dotty. I am certain they remember the time when there was only Gori and I on our morning walks.

'He used to have a dog,' I can imagine them tell newcomers to the colony. 'Then she died and he lost his balance.'

I am glad that, like me, they still remember Gori.

Epilogue

27 July 2010

The rains have come. It made the shifting more difficult than usual. Packets became wet. The skylight sprung a leak. Workers dragged dirty feet across the floors, causing Sahiba and Agnes to scream at them. The man requisitioned to hang the paintings left ugly splotches all over the walls, requiring yet another coat of paint which, in this weather, will not dry fast enough.

Still, finally, everything is mostly ready.

The curtains have been hung, the blinds work effortlessly. Agnes has taken charge of a larger, airier kitchen with another cook and a helper to assist her. The furniture is polished and shining well enough to see your face in, the way your shoes need to be polished in the army. The hanging garden in front is lush with the frequent downpours.

In the evening, people will come by for what they believe to be a housewarming party.

I have taken care to bring to the evening's menu those things that previous guests, like Gori, have enjoyed. There will be *galoutis* and *nalli korma* and *biryani.*

But what the guests do not yet know is that I intend to tell them a story.

This story.

A story which began as I opened the window, as I usually do, this morning, to overlook a patch of green and a grave marked by a tree. And ended, right here in this house, marking five years since you, Gori, went away.

It is a story of a pledge I made on the day you died, to dedicate this house to your memory no matter what it took. Nor have these five years that it took to build been easy.

The house is dedicated to the spirit of a dog that had to fight for her share of affection and space in a home that was not ready to receive her. Yet, the house is built not on a foundation of guilt, but of love. For, in truth, you know, it is nothing but a memorial to you.

I hope, my Gori, that you are happy – or at least as happy as I am today when, once again, we begin another chapter in our lives, but with one crucial difference: we will henceforth be forever in each other's sight.